AN **UNCIVIL** WAR

AN UNCIVIL WAR

TAKING BACK OUR DEMOCRACY IN AN AGE OF TRUMPIAN DISINFORMATION AND THUNDERDOME POLITICS

GREG SARGENT

 For information, address HarperCollins Publishers, 195 Broadway, New York, NY 10007.

HarperCollins books may be purchased for educational, business, or sales promotional use. For information, please email the Special Markets Department at SPsales@harpercollins.com.

FIRST EDITION

Library of Congress Cataloging-in-Publication Data has been applied for.

ISBN 978-0-06-269845-2

18 19 20 21 22 DIX/LSC 10 9 8 7 6 5 4 3 2 1

In memory of Robert Schmidt, 1928–2018

Contents

1

A Dangerous Paradox

We are living through an exceptionally fraught period in the political life of this country. And at its core is a dangerous paradox.

On the one hand, the ascension of Donald Trump to the presidency has sparked an outpouring of fear, anxiety, and introspection about the state of our democracy that is rivaled by nothing in recent memory. The Trump era intuitively *feels* to many of us as if it is saturated with a level of peril to our political system, and to the rights, liberties, and stability it guarantees, that elevates the present moment to one of profound historical consequence. It feels comparable to, say, how we now look back on the Watergate era in the 1970s; the tumult over civil rights and the Vietnam War and the urban riots and assassinations of the 1960s; or the rise of demagogue Senator Joe McCarthy in the 1950s. Trump's rise has unleashed a profound sense among both elites and well-informed rank-and-file voters—and among many citizens who were previously uninterested in political participation but suddenly find themselves more actively engaged than at any other point in their lives—that our democracy and its core institutions are under serious stress at best, and face profound or even existential peril at worst.

At the same time, the very fact that it required the rise of a singularly demagogic and menacing figure like Trump to rivet the nation's attention on the state of our democracy is itself a serious problem. To be sure, the current occupant of the Oval Office is a serial despoiler of our political system. But the plight of our democracy is the result of a series of deep structural factors and problems that go well beyond Trump, and long predate him. These problems both helped produce Trump's rise and are an essential reason this Trumpian moment is so perilous. The fact that Trump himself is the intense focal point of much of the nation's anxiety about our democracy—that it required Trump's rise to awaken our attention to the degree that it has—is symptomatic of a long-running failure to adequately grasp those problems as a cause for serious worry on their own terms.

Trump does, of course, seem to personally embody a series of challenges to our democracy that few of us expected to see in our lifetimes. His authoritarian and autocratic instincts—which he continues to unabashedly display in countless tweets, public pronouncements, and actions—are very real. They have represented a grave threat ever since his rise began, and continue to menace our political system in a manner whose consequences remain unpredictable. Throughout the 2016 campaign, Trump viciously attacked the foundational institutions of liberal democratic governance—the free press, the judiciary, the career government professionals whose technocratic expertise sustains the modern bureaucratic state. He campaigned heavily on the notion that our democratic processes themselves can no longer render legitimate outcomes. He attacked our elections as rigged and riddled with fraud, sometimes even suggesting that U.S. officials themselves were complicit in their corruption. He flatly threatened to treat the election's outcome as invalid if he lost, thus hinting that in that event he might try to disrupt the peaceful transfer of power, a hallmark of democratic stability. Trump buttressed that narrative by threatening to jail his opponent, telegraphing to his supporters that if Hillary Clinton prevailed, her presidency would be a criminal usurpation. His top campaign advisers—including those who are also close family members—demonstrated their willingness to collude with a hostile foreign power to influence the outcome of the election,[1] even though that foreign power appeared devoted to the express goal of undermining our democracy through a concerted campaign of sowing chaos and disinformation among American voters.[2] Trump himself openly urged Russia to hack into Hillary Clinton's emails,[3] in effect calling on a foreign adversary to undermine his legitimate political opponent, the nominee of one of the two major American political parties, through weaponized cyber subterfuge.

No sooner had Trump assumed office than his offensive

against the institutions of our liberal democracy, if anything, escalated. Alarmingly, those attacks appeared to be a direct response to his increasing recognition that they were functioning properly—as checks on his power. These attacks on the judiciary have continued, and his assaults on the media have taken on the cast of a systematic campaign to undermine the free press's institutional role in our democracy. He has also trampled all sorts of other democratic norms, including refusing to release his tax returns, brushing off a self-imposed standard of transparency that presidential candidates have followed for decades. (Compounding insult and injury to voters, in late 2017 he signed a tax reform package that showered enormous benefits on the wealthy, yet voters were unable to determine the worth of the benefits it lavished upon himself and his family, which likely amounted to savings of millions of dollars at a minimum.[4]) He has engaged in all manner of other self-dealing, from unabashedly profiting off events held by fellow Republicans at his hotels[5] (money spent at least in part for the express purpose of ingratiation with the president) to using the presidency to drive publicity and business to his Mar-a-Lago resort in Florida—all reinforcing a sense that he is enriching himself off the presidency and normalizing naked corruption, setting terribly damaging precedents for our democracy.[6]

The list goes on: Trump fired his FBI director and admitted on national television that he'd done it out of anger over the ongoing FBI investigation of his campaign's alleged collaboration with Russia's efforts to sabotage the

2016 presidential election on his behalf.[7] He repeatedly raged at his attorney general for failing to protect him from that probe.[8] After the appointment of a special counsel to investigate those matters, Trump escalated his war on our intelligence agencies and the Department of Justice, seeking to undermine any efforts to hold him or his family members and associates accountable in a manner straight out of the autocrat's playbook. He repeatedly considered trying to remove the special counsel—who had been focusing on his efforts to interfere with that investigation—at one point privately ordering his White House counsel to carry out the deed. (The White House counsel, Don McGahn, refused and threatened to quit, and Trump backed down.[9]) Trump has actively conspired with Republicans to weaponize Congress's investigative machinery against his own Justice Department's investigation into himself. He has largely refused to acknowledge that those Russian efforts to interfere in our election happened at all, potentially leaving us ill equipped to counter future efforts to corrupt American democracy.[10]

To be sure, it's a stretch to say that our democracy is substantially eroding when compared to other previous periods throughout our history. Certain aspects of it are eroding relative to recent years, but when you take the longer view, there have of course been periods during which things were far, far worse than they are now—periods in which corruption or civil rights abuses were rampant; periods consumed with bloody political violence, not to mention civil war; periods during which democracy simply didn't exist at all for large swaths of the population. What's more, there are reasons to be optimistic that our institutions are, while battered and black-eyed, largely holding up in the face of Trump's degradations. Yet the tally of damage that the Trump era has wrought—and continues to inflict—on our political system is simply staggering. And when most of us think about our current political moment, we think mainly about all of these Trumpian degradations. But the very fact that we have seen this sudden pileup of burdens itself hints that focusing only on Trump as the catalyst is highly insufficient. How is it possible that one man could suddenly step forward and single-handedly subject our democracy to so much stress and potential peril?

The answer to that question has less to do with Donald Trump than the constant crush of anguished media attention to every Trumpian rage-tweet, racist slur, authoritarian-accented threat, and expression of seething contempt for our institutions makes it seem.

Democratic Backsliding

In each national election, tens of millions of us go to the polls and choose a number of people to represent us in the national government. The story we tell ourselves about this ritual is fairly straightforward. We have spent days or weeks or months leading up to election day evaluating the public statements and policy positions of competing candidates, delivered to us by our preferred news media and information sources, most of which (we have generally believed) are making a good-faith effort to inform us about the choice we face. Generally speaking, many of us cast a ballot in the firm expectation that each of our votes will carry equal weight, and that the candidate or party that receives a majority of votes will prevail. If more Americans cast their vote for Democratic candidates for the House of Representatives, then the Democratic Party will control that chamber of Congress; if more Americans vote for Republicans, then the Republican Party will control it. The same, many of us assume, goes for our state and local legislatures. While there have been plenty of individual instances in which the party that narrowly received the most votes ultimately fell short of winning control of the legislative body in question, surely many voters have not traditionally thought of this as typical. And while it's true that the president is selected by the Electoral College, a lot of Americans likely regard this as largely an anachronism, and have generally anticipated that the winner will almost always be the one who captures the most votes. In short, many of us have long viewed our democracy as, generally speaking, a flawed but functional and fair system of majority rule. But many analysts had begun to warn—even well in advance of Trump's appearance on the political scene, back when most Americans were only dimly aware of Trump as a distant, shriveled, cartoonish reality-

TV figure, if they knew of him at all—that the story we tell ourselves about our political system is growing more difficult to sustain, due to a confluence of factors.

Political scientists have a term for the weakening or degeneration of democracy: *democratic backsliding*. One of the most prominent theorists of democratic backsliding, Nancy Bermeo, a political scientist at Princeton University, has defined the phenomenon as occurring when lawmakers or political actors engage in the "debilitation or elimination of any of the political institutions that sustain an existing democracy." It's a broad term, because the process can take a wide range of forms. At the outer extreme of the range are things like classic coups, in which a legitimately elected political figure is violently ousted; executive coups, in which a democratically elected leader suspends his country's constitution to amass vastly greater or unchecked power; and straight-up stolen elections, in which leaders install themselves through blatant and widespread election fraud. A more gradual version of democratic backsliding, in Bermeo's taxonomy, is what she terms *executive aggrandizement*. This occurs when an elected executive slowly consolidates power, not through abrupt suspensions of the existing constitutional order, but rather through the systematic weakening—via legal processes—of institutions that act as a check on that power. A still more gradual version of democratic backsliding is *strategic harassment and manipulation*. This phenomenon, Bermeo notes, comprises a "range of actions aimed at tilting the electoral playing field," including tactics such as "hampering voter registration," or "changing electoral rules to favor incumbents," or "harassing opponents."

In recent years, all of these forms of democratic backsliding have been on display in many countries around the world. But the good news is that the most blatant forms of it have been on the decline. Classic and executive coups were common during the Cold War but are rarely seen today. Widespread election fraud is also on the decline. But the more subtle forms of backsliding, unfortunately, are on the rise. International observers have noted that forms of executive consolidation of power have taken place in many countries, even as they have also registered an uptick in strategic manipulation and harassment. The upshot of this, as Bermeo has concluded, is that "de-democratization today tends to be incremental rather than sudden."

In other words, the main threat to democracy in the contemporary world is gradual, multicausal, sustained deterioration or erosion. But this recognition brings with it a fresh set of challenges. One of these is how to identify and measure that deterioration when it is taking place. Another is identifying the causes of that deterioration—what or who is to blame for it, and in the cases where specific actors are indeed to blame, what incentives and motives are encouraging their behavior. Still another is what to do to reverse these trends. All of these turn out to be much more complex and difficult problems than you might think. Scholars and analysts are increasingly preoccupied by them. And as a result, they are rethinking fundamental questions about how and why democracies decline. As Bermeo puts it:

> Focusing on democratic erosion will require more scholars to see that democracy is "a collage" of institutions crafted and recrafted by different actors at different times. It is put together piece by piece, and can be taken apart the same way.[11]

In recent years, scholars and analysts have also become preoccupied with the question of whether this is occurring in America.

We can measure the health or sickness of a democracy—the health or sickness of a body politic—by looking at its vital signs. But it turns out that establishing what these vital signs are—that is, establishing what should be measured in the first place, let alone how to measure them—is a very complicated business. As one group of scholars recently lamented in a comprehensive examination of various efforts to measure how democratic any given political system is, "no consensus has emerged about how to conceptualize and measure this key concept." This is a problem, they concluded, because "if we cannot measure democracy in some fashion we cannot mark its progress and setbacks."[12]

One creative and comprehensive response to this challenge has been crafted by a group of political scientists at Yale University, Dartmouth College, and the University of Rochester. Their project, which is called Bright Line Watch, offers a set of concrete and specific metrics for gauging the strength of our democratic practices and their resilience in the face of stresses on them. By regularly surveying several hundred political scientists from around the country, they can derive a consensus among them on the state of the nation. On some dimensions that are crucial to maintaining democracy—such as whether our elections are largely free of fraud, and whether free speech and the rights of protest and association are broadly respected—our democracy is ranked as being quite healthy. But in a number of other areas, the democratic performance of our system is wanting. These experts give our democracy lackluster to low ratings on questions such as whether voting rights are equal, whether our votes have equal impact, whether political participation is robust, whether our elections are free of foreign influence, whether electoral districts are neutrally drawn, and even whether our political actors are motivated by the basic goal of compromise and whether they are operating from a common understanding of facts.[13] As the Bright Line Watch project put it in an overview of one recent set of expert assessments, there is "pessimism" among scholars about our democracy in these dimensions when measured against "international standards," with most other democracies producing "clearly better results on these items" than ours.[14]

To be sure, there are many other ways to identify and measure the vital signs of our democracy, and there are threats to democracy that the Bright Line Watch does not reckon with, from fraying social bonds to stagnant economic growth and rising economic inequality. But for now the important point to understand is that our democracy's health or sickness can be gauged in part by evaluating its performance in very specific areas. And there is a remarkable degree of consensus among political scientists right now about the relative weakness of our democracy on all of those particular fronts listed above.

What about the larger American public? Well, lots of Americans also think something has gone very, very wrong. A Pew Research poll taken in October 2016, amid the final, frenzied days of the viciously fought presidential contest, found that only 32 percent of voters had a great deal of confidence that the election would be "open and fair."[15] A Public Religion Research Survey taken at around the same time found that only 43 percent of Americans had a great deal of confidence that their votes would be counted accurately.[16] Nearly one year after the election, in September 2017, the Bright Line Watch team undertook a comprehensive study of thousands of American voters and found that they were, on balance, "quite concerned" and even "alarmed" about the "health of U.S. democracy" in a number of dimensions, giving our system low ratings over things like the lack of transparency into the funding of campaigns, the biased drawing of electoral districts, and low voter participation in elections.[17] More broadly, public trust in government itself has steadily declined in the last two decades. According to data tabulated by the Pew Research Center, the percentage of Americans who trust the government in Washington all or most of the time is hovering at a historic nadir, languishing below the 20 percent mark.[18]

This sort of declining faith in democracy may represent more than mere public awareness of its deep problems; it may itself pose a threat to its durability. In an essay about democratic backsliding in Western democracies, the Harvard University political theorist Pippa Norris noted that "deep disenchantment with the workings of political institutions, like elections and legislatures, may have destabilizing effects upon the body politic, opening the door to populist demagogues" who seize on this disillusionment to further undermine faith in other institutions crucial to liberal democracy, such as the courts and the free and independent press.[19]

We have, of course, seen precisely this tactic from the populist demagogue known as Donald J. Trump. In this sense, Trump appears to be trying to carry out his own version of one of the forms of democratic backsliding noted above, *executive aggrandizement*—that is to say, the consolidation of power via efforts to weaken institutions that constrain it and function as bulwarks of accountability.

The Case for Alarmism

At this point, well into the Trump presidency, many democratic theorists have now documented serious and meaningful parallels between Trump's behavior and that of autocrats who have successfully wielded such tactics to engineer democratic backsliding in their countries. Steven Levitsky and Daniel Ziblatt, professors of government at Harvard, argued in their 2018 book, *How Democracies Die*, that Trump's presidency has already exhibited many of the telltale signs of an impending autocratic takeover, and that his ascension should be all the more alarming because the "guardrails" of democracy, which are supposed to protect the system against such autocratic encroachment, are right now perilously weak.[20] They argue for what one might call the "unexceptionalism" of American democracy, meaning that, as they put it, our system is "vulnerable to the same pathologies that have killed democracy elsewhere." Somewhat more optimistically, a trio of political thinkers—*Washington Post* columnist E. J. Dionne Jr. and political scientists Norman J. Ornstein and Thomas E. Mann—argued in their book *One Nation After Trump* that Trump's rise has created an extended crisis for our democracy, but that this crisis has activated a deep and reinvigorated civic faith that could yet prove its salvation.[21] Meanwhile, Robert R. Kaufman and Stephan Haggard—professors of political science at Rutgers University and the University of California, San Diego who have spent many years studying the reversion of democratic states—have concluded that Trump's behavior does indeed echo that of other successful autocrats, in that he has systematically sought to weaken institutional constraints that threaten to impose accountability or function as a check on his power.[22]

In these accounts, there are grounds for both optimism

and pessimism. On the positive side, Trump's efforts in this regard have yet to succeed by the standards of other autocratic takeovers—they have not yet come close. Most signs are that Trump's assaults on critical institutions have not meaningfully weakened them as checks on his power. While the Republican-controlled Congress has not exercised nearly the oversight it should have toward Trump's self-dealing and corruption (a topic we will return to later in this book), it has at times acted as a limiting force. His attacks on law enforcement have done some damage, but they have not derailed the Justice Department's ongoing investigation of the Russian effort to sabotage our democracy and Trump campaign collusion with it. The news media, if anything, has intensified its scrutiny of the president and his administration. There are reasons to believe our institutions have in key ways proven robust and resilient.

But on the negative side, what all these accounts also share—an assessment reached in many other articles and scholarly papers and podcasts and so forth—is that Trump's presidency is hastening what has been a longer-term deterioration of informal political norms, with potentially severe and lasting consequences. These norms, which have occupied a great deal of attention of late, are the wide range of mostly unwritten rules that in functional democracies constrain lawmakers and party officials from allowing politics to devolve into an outright power struggle in which anything goes. Most observers agree, as Kaufman and Haggard conclude, that the norms that are further eroding in the

Trump era "had long been a bulwark of democratic stability in the United States," and that this erosion is deepening the divisions in our politics. As Kaufman and Haggard put it, the result is an increasing tendency on the part of both elites and groups of mass voters "to set a lower priority on fair democratic procedures than on preventing a victory of the other side." These changing priorities are visible in rising restrictions on voting rights and other tactics designed to render elections less competitive, and in the increasing depiction of political opponents as fundamentally illegitimate, which in turn justifies those tactics in a kind of downward, self-reinforcing spiral.[23]

In this pessimistic spirit, a team of political scientists from Cornell University, Johns Hopkins University, and Swarthmore College released an analysis in August 2017 that is only more starkly relevant today. In it, they bluntly warned of a confluence of factors weakening democracy in the era of Trump—including the growing power of the presidency and deepening polarization along partisan and racial lines over fundamental questions such as who belongs in the American political community (another topic we will develop later). They, too, declared "commonly held but often informal understandings that govern behavior" as crucial to enabling our political system's "smooth functioning and long-term stability." In a political system such as ours, which features power dispersed among different branches and levels of government, along with "veto points" where "policy change can be blocked or frustrated," demolishing such "informal understandings" could prove more and more destabilizing, as the two parties increasingly manipulate those features of our system to their own partisan ends, placing our institutions at ever greater risk of being "manipulated and turned into instruments of partisan advantage."[24]

In this book, I hope to tell the story of this degeneration by drilling down on the concept of fair play in politics. Even now, the very idea of what constitutes fair play in politics, as well as what threatens it, is deeply contested, and will continue to be subject to intense partisan disagreement. It can even seem as if political fair play is a pipe dream, that fair play is fundamentally incompatible with political competition—a feeling that right now is especially understandable. Should partisans even bother to strive toward an ideal of fair play to begin with? Why not just accept that politics is a naked power struggle and act accordingly? The latter conclusion will no doubt be a very tempting one for those who are watching Trump and Republicans stomp all over any such ideal of fair play—and are gaming out what will happen once they can be ousted from power and replaced.

Fair Play in Politics: Two Separate Realities

If you spend a fair amount of time closely following politics, particularly on social media, you'll find there are basically two separate realities. The first, subscribed to by many Republican voters and some conservative opinion makers, is that our elections are deeply compromised by the fraudulent impersonation of voters. In this telling, Democrats regularly undertake organized efforts to engineer voting in their favor by large numbers of undocumented immigrants, or people who, ineligible to vote, impersonate those whose names are on the rolls. The second, subscribed to by many Democratic voters and some liberal opinion makers, is that our elections are compromised by a combination of voter suppression, the gerrymandering of congressional maps, Electoral College distortion, and underhanded GOP tactics. In this telling, Republicans have largely held their grip on power through laws that deliberately make it hard for minorities and other Democratic-leaning constituencies to vote, and by redrawing congressional districts so that they have retained an unbreakable grip on the House of Representatives, insulating GOP lawmakers from broader currents of national majority opinion and allowing them to embrace policies that are out of step with it.

Polling reveals this deep split between perceptions of these two realities. A *Washington Post* poll in September 2016 found that over two thirds of Trump supporters thought voter fraud occurred often, while fewer than one third of Clinton supporters believed that.[25] A Public Religion Research Institute poll in October 2016 found that two thirds of Republican voters believed voter fraud was a bigger problem than the disenfranchisement of voters—but 62 percent of Democrats said eligible people being denied voting access was the bigger problem.[26] These sorts of divides persisted after the election. Trump repeatedly declared that he would have won the popular vote if not for millions of people who voted illegally. He offered no evidence of any kind for this claim, but many Republican voters continue to believe him: One June 2017 poll found that 47 percent of Republicans thought Trump won the popular vote, and a whopping 73 percent said voter fraud happens somewhat or very often.[27] (Both of these are false.) Meanwhile, a post-election *Economist*/YouGov poll found that half of Clinton voters believed the Russian government successfully hacked the vote count in Trump's favor.[28] (Which is also false.)

This divergence doesn't end here. The first version of political reality—the one subscribed to by many Republican voters and some conservative opinion makers—also holds that because Democratic electoral victories are fueled by massive vote fraud and because Democratic policies tend to increase taxes and welfare spending, they represent something akin to a confiscation and redistribution of wealth via fraudulent means. Democrats thus effectively buy the allegiance of their voters (fraudulent and otherwise) with other people's money, further compounding the illegitimacy of their electoral victories and the policies they enact. The political theorist Will Wilkinson has pointed out that there is a long tradition on the right that links the belief in the illegitimacy of redistributive policies with skepticism about the legitimacy of democracy itself. In this telling, Wilkinson notes, democracy is sometimes seen as a "mechanism for some people to gang up on other people" and "steal their stuff" in an act of "institutionalized theft." Once this is accepted, Democratic electoral victories and the policies that result from them then become deeply suspect.[29]

The second reality—the one subscribed to by many Democratic voters and a fair amount of liberal opinion makers—also holds that GOP lawmakers have basically broken our political system by embracing a series of scorched-earth governing tactics. Republicans have relentlessly staked out new frontiers in political dishonesty and bad faith in misrepresenting their actual policy goals; they have systematically attacked neutral referees (such as the press and nonpartisan analytical agencies) when their conclusions about the impact of Republican policies were unflattering. And they have shattered basic norms of fair play with tactics such as the unprecedented obstruction of Democratic legislation and appointments when in the Senate minority, and the refusal to give a hearing to one of Barack Obama's nominees to the Supreme Court when they were in the Senate majority.

The second of these two diagnoses, this book will argue, is far closer to the mark. Voter suppression and extreme gerrymandering—perpetrated mostly by Republicans—are hideously undemocratic practices, while voter fraud is largely a fiction. Republican assaults on our democratic and governing norms really have been more destructive than Democratic ones have been. Republicans have demonstrated a level of bad faith in misrepresenting their policy goals and in the undermining of nonpartisan referees—and the independent press—that just hasn't been present to anywhere near the same degree on the Democratic side. None of this is to say that Democrats are completely innocent; there's plenty of blame for the current state of our politics to go around. Still, without a doubt Republicans have done a lot more damage than Democrats have done. And knitting all of that damage together is the fact that some of these tactics really are driven by a broader GOP goal of entrenching minority rule. While the GOP does benefit from already existing structural advantages—as will be discussed later—they have also employed overt countermajoritarian means toward the end of further exploiting and exacerbating those advantages. As Jonathan Chait, a liberal writer for *New York* magazine, put it, you cannot understand the GOP's embrace of Trump's many excesses without appreciating the degree to which the party has grown "increasingly comfortable with, and reliant on, countermajoritarian power."[30]

But while all of this is a big part of the story, our challenge is also to understand the deeper forces that are leading to the profusion of these tactics, why there is a rising incentive for certain political actors to engage in them, and what explains the increasing divergence in perceptions of political reality itself. Then we must ask how all these factors enabled Trump's rise, how they are rendering the Trump era particularly dangerous to our democracy, how they might outlast Trump and continue getting worse, and what might be done to fight back. It is the contention of this book that addressing all of these things is eminently achievable in one way or another, even if right now that appears rather hopeless. And while plenty of other dire threats to our democracy are ever-present (the flood of big outside money; the threat of foreign election hacking; and so on) this is where our task begins.

Right now, that task is particularly urgent, because we are heading into a series of elections in which the stakes appear to be exceptionally high. The 2018 midterm congressional elections and the 2020 presidential and congressional elections will constitute referendums not just on Trump and his brand of race-baiting, authoritarian politics, but also on how successfully our political system can hold up under the strains that the Trump era has brought to bear on it. Among the big questions we face:

- As president, Trump has continued to attack the legitimacy of our elections. He has even raised doubts about the legitimacy of the upcoming midterms. Will that disillusion voters in any way that appreciably diminishes participation and voter turnout? What will be the lasting fallout of his extensive efforts to cast our political system as irredeemably corrupt in the minds of millions of his supporters?
- GOP voter suppression efforts will continue—and even escalate—and they have been explicitly endorsed by Trump, who has used his bully pulpit to aggressively promote lies about voter fraud to a much greater

degree than any previous president. Will those efforts disenfranchise Democratic voters in the midterms, potentially costing them seats? How much worse will the tactics get over time?

- Some of our current extreme gerrymanders—created mostly but not exclusively by Republicans—will remain in place for at least the next two elections. Will they enable Republicans to hold the House even if they lose the popular vote? Will they further entrench countermajoritarian GOP rule?
- Trump's nonstop lying has flooded our politics with a level of disinformation that may be unprecedented, and we may see Russia wage more information warfare in upcoming elections, no doubt encouraged in part by Trump's refusal to take Russian interference seriously. Will news organizations be able to adapt to new and very difficult challenges posted by what appears to be a deeply perilous new information landscape? Will the gales of disinformation battering our politics have a real impact on electoral outcomes?

This book will try to address all these questions and problems—and more.

Thunderdome Politics

Not only has Trump hastened the ongoing degradation of our politics in all kinds of incalculable ways—constantly flooding the media zone with blustery pronouncements, grotesque exercises in misdirection, flagrant distortions, staggeringly audacious lies, openly racist provocations, and all-around political trash talk of the rankest kind—but he has debased and corrupted our discourse, and with it, our ability to deliberate in a nonhysterical, lower-volume way about all these degradations. While this particular deterioration is hardly Trump's doing alone, he has built upon continuing trends with a political style that, by instinct or design, combines quasi-totalitarian propaganda techniques with a former reality TV star's grasp of our rapidly shifting media and information environment (a topic we'll take up at greater length later), exacerbating our political system's increasingly full-blown partisan warfare (a process under way for all kinds of reasons) into the crudest of politics-as-blood-sport entertainment. Bearing witness to it all can sometimes feel like watching the gladiatorial combat in the Thunderdome, the arena in the 1985 movie *Mad Max Beyond Thunderdome*, in which conflicts were resolved by hand-to-hand fights to the death, with maximum-pain-inflicting weapons that hang inside the Thunderdome itself, creating the opportunity to perpetrate horrors for spectators outside, who are inhabitants of a postapocalyptic dystopia. I write a blog for *The Washington Post*, called The Plum Line, which is about the unsightly horrors that take place, day in and day out, in our Thunderdome politics. I trust that I'm speaking for others who write about our politics regularly when I say that there is often a temptation to chronicle ongoing events in a smashmouth tone that captures the ugly spirit of these overall degradations. But what will happen to our politics after this particular sequel ends? What trends will remain with us, and what will their long-term damage be? These questions require a more sedate effort to supply a bigger-picture perspective—and an effort to reclaim our discourse from the Thunderdome as well. I hope this book succeeds in making its own modest contribution to this genre, which has already seen many other important contributions.

It seems increasingly easy to envision scenarios in which the Trump presidency passes—having done a fair amount of damage, but without bringing about the precipitous slide into autocracy that many feared at the outset of it. Yet the factors and problems eroding our democracy long predate the current president—and will outlast him. The focus on Trump as the chief threat underscores our failure to reckon with those maladies. To return to the paradox outlined at the beginning of this chapter: It required the rise of an outsize, menacing figure with openly demonstrated contempt for our democracy—one who has been overtly engaged in efforts to undermine it in all kinds of ways—to activate widespread public concern about the viability and durability of our political system. Once we have gotten past our current moment, will we retain memories of the alarm Trump's rise sounded, and act to improve our political system when we have another chance to do so? Or will the deep public concern about our democracy that Trump ushered in simply dissipate and allow the more insidious forms of damage to continue eating away at it unchecked, until things degenerate to a point that is incalculably worse?

2

Voter Suppression: Into the Partisan Vortex

It is tempting to believe that over the course of American history, the story of access to the ballot has been a uniform tale of slow and seamless expansion. Certainly that's the feel-good version we often teach to our children, that one group after another inexorably gained the right to vote until universal suffrage was achieved amid the civil rights revolution of the second half of the twentieth century. But the true tale is much more complicated and a good deal less inspiring. It isn't just that we didn't have anything close to full participatory democracy for nearly two centuries after the country's founding. It's also that in reality, the franchise has gone through protracted contractions *after* periods of expansion. Not only has progress in voting access been very hard won, but it has often been met with major setbacks, reversals, and periods of terrible backsliding. In some cases, groups that had previously gained expanded political rights subsequently lost them.

The framers of the Constitution opted to delegate to the state legislatures the power to set rules involving the timing, location, and manner of elections for members of Congress, while also reserving for Congress the power to later step in and set or change those rules. This provision was the result of much intense debate. On one side were those who wanted to reserve authority to the states, out of fears that a tyrannical national government would manipulate the rules to entrench its own power. On the other were those who wanted Congress to be able to override the states, out of fear that state legislatures might manipulate the rules to entrench *their* own power, in ways that would compromise representation of the people's interests. This last group included James Madison, who gave a speech warning that state legislatures might resort to "abuses" of election rules that would help the chances of passing any particular "favorite measure" or would "favor the candidates they wished to succeed." (This is precisely what we see today.) The result was a compromise that was designed to prevent states from objecting and sinking the whole Constitution.[1] In the end, Article 1, Section 4 of the Constitution read as follows:

> The Times, Places, and Manner of holding Elections for Senators and Representatives, shall be prescribed in each State by the Legislature thereof; but the Congress may at any time by Law make or alter such Regulations, except as to the Places of Chusing Senators.

Yet, while this did reserve for the national government the power to step in and alter the rules, it left a great deal of discretion to the states to set them. What's more, the Constitution did not establish a "positive right to vote," or "set the criteria for the exercise of the franchise," as Stanford University historian Jack Rakove puts it, another decision that was in effect "defaulted to the states." This allowed the states great latitude to place restrictions on voting that amounted to efforts to determine *who* got to vote. As Harvard University historian Alexander Keyssar has written, the Constitution "left the federal government without any clear power or mechanism, other than through constitutional amendment, to institute a national conception of voting rights." Instead, "the individual states retained the power to define just who 'the people' were," a fact that "was to have significant repercussions for almost two centuries."[2]

Those repercussions have manifested themselves in a saga that has zigged and zagged and lurched forward and backward. From the 1790s through the start of the Civil War, the basic story of access to the ballot—at least for white men—was one of expansion; virtually all states had eliminated property requirements by the 1850s. Yet over this period, states that had permitted free African Americans to vote during the independence years restricted voting to whites, and the number of states that formally denied the vote to free African Americans increased. Native Americans saw their ability to vote slowly whittled down by the courts and by states who judged them to be not legally white (and thus unfit to vote). It is a little-known historical fact that in the early and middle nineteenth century, some states granted the vote to foreign-born aliens who had lived in the United States for a brief period and intended to become citizens; but alien suffrage was eventually phased out later in the nineteenth century and into the early twentieth century. In some states, even immigrants who did secure citizenship saw their access to the ballot limited amid rising anti-immigrant Know-Nothingism, measures that were sometimes justified on the grounds that they would reduce fraud (an argument we'll be hearing a lot about later in this book).

African Americans, of course, suffered a similar fate in far more dramatic and horrible fashion. After the Fifteenth Amendment granted the right to vote to African Americans (who had only just been recently liberated from slavery)—which they celebrated by marching in parades around the country—voting access and participation soared. Many were elected to public office during the Reconstruction period. But this was followed by violent reactionary blowback in the decades that followed. Then, with Congress backing away from efforts to enforce the Fifteenth Amendment, what followed was a massive lurch backward. From 1890 through around 1915, many southern states used a combination of tactics—such as poll taxes and literacy tests—to disenfranchise blacks without expressly violating the Fifteenth Amendment. (These measures were upheld by the Supreme Court.) The tactics worked: black electoral participation plummeted sharply throughout the South and remained abysmally low for many decades throughout the twentieth century.

The drive for women's suffrage was famously launched at a convention at Seneca Falls, New York, in 1848, but many who were pushing for the vote for African Americans feared that cause would be hampered by simultaneous pursuit of the vote for women. The movement for women's suffrage dragged on for many decades, with activists trying to gain the right to vote via referenda in many states but failing more often than they succeeded. That men were reluctant to grant women the right to vote in the late nineteenth century reflected a waning of enthusiasm for the idea of voting as a *right* (which had been a more common attitude during the flourishing of "Jacksonian democracy" in the 1830s and 1840s) and a resurgence of the view of voting as a *privilege*, which in a sense represented another form of backsliding. It wasn't until the performance of women during the mobilization for World War I, combined with other major social changes that fundamentally shifted gender roles—and a mass suffrage movement involving millions of people—that passage of the Nineteenth Amendment was achieved in 1920, nearly doubling the size of the electorate.

Even so, it was only decades later, in the 1960s, that anything approaching true universal suffrage was achieved. The civil and voting rights revolutions of the 1960s, spurred on by years of pressure brought to bear on elected leaders by marchers who braved violence and death, and a series of court decisions and acts by Congress—including one of the towering achievements of the civil rights era, the Voting Rights Act of 1965, which enforced the Fifteenth Amendment's prohibition on state measures abridging the right to vote on account of race, and required some states and localities to get federal preclearance for changes in voting rules—finally made the right to vote for African Americans a reality, nearly two centuries after the signing of the Declaration of Independence.[3]

In his famous 1965 speech to Congress just several months before passage of the Voting Rights Act, President Lyndon B. Johnson dramatically shouted that "we shall overcome," signaling that voting reform was on its way, and many in the audience applauded and cheered wildly and stamped their feet.[4] Martin Luther King Jr., watching the speech on television in a living room in Selma, Alabama, wept.[5] Black voter registration once again soared. But in the period that followed, the power of the vote itself came under attack by other tactics, such as voter suppression and gerrymandering (to be discussed later). Those attacks have continued, resulting in a protracted era of intense, at times racially charged fighting over the ballot that consumes us today.

The Modern Voting Wars

Republicans and Democrats inhabit different political realities, as mentioned in the previous chapter. But there are certain facts about our politics that are just objectively true. One of them is this: Generally speaking, efforts to make it harder to vote are almost always pushed by Republicans. You cannot understand what is happening in American politics right now without recognizing this stark and very fundamental difference between the two major political parties. During this decade, procedural hurdles were put in place in around twenty states that, in some manner or other, have made it harder to vote or register to vote, or have undone previous efforts to make voting or registering easier, or have otherwise threatened serious disenfranchisement. Most of them were the creation of Republican lawmakers and officials. The difference in the two parties' national platforms for 2016 tells the story: the GOP platform champions additional hurdles that are absurdly disproportionate to the phantom "abuse" it alleges, while the Democratic platform champions multiple specific ways to make it "easier to vote, not harder."[6]

The most common—and controversial—of measures used by Republicans to suppress Democratic turnout is the requirement that would-be voters present identification at the polls. The game here tends to turn on requiring forms of ID that some groups are less likely to have, making participation harder for them. Other restrictions include techniques like cutting back on early voting and making it harder to register—both of which have in recent years been instituted in multiple states. Republicans who have passed laws making it harder to vote have tended to claim such measures are necessary to protect against "voter fraud." We will look at this in more detail below, but for now, note that most of the states that have passed such measures did so while under Republican control. As New York University political scientist Samuel Issacharoff has memorably put it, "the single predictor necessary to determine whether a state will impose voter-access restrictions is whether Republicans control the ballot access process."[7]

Scholars trace the modern era of warfare over election rules to the intensely contested presidential election of 2000, in which a divided Supreme Court halted the recount in Florida, throwing the presidency to George W. Bush. The closeness and partisan acrimony of that contest, combined with the intense national focus on election rules that accompanied the court battle over it, helped persuade both parties to invest much more attention and energy on those rules. As a result, both the implementation of measures restricting the ballot and the legal battles over them have intensified in recent years.

A brief glance at the surprising history of voter ID laws begins to tell the story of this tightening. In the 1970s several states implemented voter ID measures, but all of them provided for ways that voters without the proper ID could cast a ballot.[8] By 2000 there were fourteen such laws, and they had been implemented by politicians in both parties. But in the mid-2000s, amid rising post-2000 acrimony, a handful of red states began implementing voter ID laws that the nonpartisan National Conference of State Legislatures describes as "strict"—meaning they make it easy to disqualify those who don't pass muster. After one of those laws—in Indiana—was challenged and then upheld in 2008 by the Supreme Court, an escalation began that gained momentum in the Obama era. From 2010 onward, the adoption of voter ID laws in general—and of strict ones in particular—accelerated. Though a handful were blocked in the courts, as of this writing, a total of thirty-four states have voter ID laws in effect, twenty-four that are deemed "nonstrict" and ten that are deemed "strict."[9] The "strict" ones are in red states or in swing states where they were implemented mainly by Republicans.

The story is very similar if you evaluate the states' voting rules in a broader way—by including not just voter ID measures, but also cutbacks to early voting and restrictions on registration. Here the trend is just as pronounced. After the 2010 elections, the Brennan Center for Justice documented a sharp rise in efforts to pass such measures in state legislatures across the country. Not all these efforts bore fruit, but many did: By the time the voting took place on election day 2016, some fourteen states had these new restrictions in place for the first time in a presidential election. Now, as of this writing, by the Brennan Center's count, some twenty states have successfully implemented either "strict" voter ID requirements, or cutbacks to early voting, or restrictions on registration, or other measures with meaningful disenfranchising effects.[10]

Voter Suppression: The Greatest Hits

If you are a liberal who is frustrated by the seemingly unbreakable Republican dominance of national politics—not to mention GOP control of most state governments across the country—then the chances are that these restrictions figure heavily into your explanation of this GOP supremacy. Indeed, social media has been absolutely saturated in recent years with variations of the lament that Republican political dominance is largely maintained through a combination of nefarious and undemocratic tactics, such as ballot restrictions that keep constituencies unfriendly to the GOP from voting, and extreme gerrymanders that have in effect built a fortress around the GOP's majority in the House of Representatives. Democrats frequently invoke the GOP's use of these tactics—often justifiably—to raise money and to galvanize turnout.

This narrative contains some important truths. Some of the forms that these restrictions on voting access have taken in recent years are diabolically obvious in their efforts to keep constituencies supportive of Democrats from voting. Still others boast the distinction of being more insidiously designed and thus less obvious in their intentions. To be fair, the story is in some ways more complicated than is commonly thought. Voting restrictions are not uniformly about suppressing the vote, and the broad impact on participation of these measures is the subject of legitimate dispute (a topic that will be addressed later). Still, efforts to restrict access to the vote take on an outsize role in this broad account of continued GOP supremacy for a good reason: the most glaring examples of them are truly shocking and justifiably command extensive public and media attention. Indeed, at times, they are almost cartoonish in their mustache-twiddling, back-room-chortling villainy. In the most common version of this, legislators pass requirements that voters show ID at the polls—a hurdle that isn't necessarily problematic in and of itself, depending on how it is applied—with the deliberate end of making it harder for only the other party's voters to cast ballots. In so doing, legislators manipulate the rules to entrench themselves and their party in power.

It is remarkable how blatant this scheme has been in certain cases, and it is no accident that the most glaring examples of this came right after the Supreme Court's notorious ruling striking down a key piece of the Voting Rights Act in its 2013 decision, *Shelby County, Alabama v. Holder*. That decision gutted the section of the law determining which states and localities—ones with a history of discrimination in voting procedure—must get "preclearance" from the federal government or a court for changes to voting laws. In Texas, Republican legislators had in 2011 passed an extremely strict voter ID law allowing handgun licenses to be used as ID but not student IDs and state or federal government employee IDs. The Texas law was blocked under the Voting Rights Act, but after the high court's ruling Texas officials began implementing it. Nonetheless, a federal judge subsequently struck down the law, concluding that it deliberately facilitated voting by whites (who disproportionately own handgun licenses) while expressly seeking to limit voting by Democratic-leaning constituencies, such as young people (who disproportionately carry student IDs) and African Americans and Hispanics (who disproportionately carry government and state and federal employee IDs). As detailed below, the law survived in modified form.

Then there's North Carolina's notorious voter suppression law, an exquisitely crafted specimen of legislative cynicism. In 2013, GOP lawmakers passed a raft of voting restrictions, including a strict voter ID measure, the elimination of same-day voter registration and a dramatic reduction of permissible days for early voting. A federal appeals court struck down the law in 2016, concluding that its provisions "target African Americans with almost surgical precision." The ruling noted that well before sending the bill to the Republican governor, legislators had requested data that demonstrated the types of photo ID that African Americans disproportionately lacked, and kept that "race data in hand" as they crafted the law, in order to "exclude many of the alternative photo IDs used by African Americans," while retaining "only the kinds of IDs that white North Carolinians were more likely to possess." What's more, since African Americans were more likely to avail themselves of early voting and Sunday voting, GOP legislators naturally slashed the early voting period and clipped Sunday voting, too. This, the court found, proved "discriminatory intent" with evidence that "comes as close to a smoking gun as we are likely to see in modern times." The Supreme Court in May 2017 declined to hear an appeal of that decision, effectively invalidating the law.

Predictably, Republicans in North Carolina and those from other states who cheered them on continue to pretend that the restrictions have nothing to do with excluding nonwhites and thus depressing the Democratic vote. But there have been times when Republicans have admitted the intent behind such laws with startling clarity. After Florida Republicans passed a 2011 law cutting down early voting, leading to insufferably long lines on election day in 2012, the former chairman of the Florida Republican Party admitted to *The Palm Beach Post* that the cutbacks were "done for one reason and one reason only," and that was to rig the rules in the GOP's favor. "The Republican Party, the strategists, the consultants, they firmly believe that early voting is bad for Republican Party candidates," he explained. Though select Florida Republicans denied this, noting that the former GOP chair was under indictment at the time, another GOP consultant who spoke to the paper confirmed that suppressing Democratic votes was indeed the motive. Remarkably, this consultant explicitly admitted that such tactics were a reaction to the large turnout of Democratic constituencies that Republicans had begun to see—and fear—in the 2008 election, when Barack Obama's victory drove up turnout among minorities and young voters.[11]

Such admirable candor has been on display on other occasions as well. In Pennsylvania, a GOP legislative leader claimed in June 2012 that a recently enacted voter ID law would enable GOP presidential candidate Mitt Romney to "win the state of Pennsylvania" against then president Barack Obama.[12] In Wisconsin, where Republican legislators had passed a strict 2011 voter ID law, a former aide to one GOP lawmaker asserted in 2016 that he had sat in on a private meeting at which legislators were "giddy" about using the law to suppress Democratic votes. Even more remarkably, he claimed that one of these lawmakers had argued it would have an impact on voting in "the neighborhoods around Milwaukee" and on "college campuses," which appeared to be a reference to trying to depress voting among nonwhite and young voters.[13]

A Losing Game

In the course of writing this book, I held conversations with voting rights lawyers that frequently brought to mind a famous episode of the hit 1950s situation comedy *I Love Lucy*. The plucky, audacious star of the show and her best friend Ethel get jobs on a candy factory assembly line. Their task is to wrap chocolates as they flow past on a conveyor belt. Their boss warns them that if a single chocolate gets past them unwrapped, they will be fired. At first Lucy and Ethel have little trouble keeping pace. "Oh, this is easy," Lucy says. "Yeah, we can handle this okay," Ethel replies. But then the conveyor belt speeds up, and the volume of chocolates coming at them grows increasingly overwhelming. The two women—unable to wrap the candies fast enough—begin shoving large handfuls of them into their mouths. Lucy even stashes some in her bra. "Listen, Ethel!" Lucy shouts. "I think we're fighting a losing game!"

Lawyers who battle voter suppression in the courts sometimes sound as if they have been suffering through the legal equivalent of what Lucy and Ethel endured—albeit for years and years on end. It isn't just that the frequency and volume of these tactics have been increasing in magnitude. It's also that the frequency and volume of the legal battles over them have been escalating as well.

Not all the news here is grim: Legal battles against some of the most ingenious voter suppression tactics can boast of real successes. As noted earlier, the recent measures employed by Republicans in North Carolina have been blocked by the courts for the time being, after long struggles that involved both sustained legal battles and broad popular mobilization. Legal action also forced a revision to Texas's appalling legislation. Not all of the success is due to the courts. Popular outcry (most visible in North Carolina, where protests rocked the state) drew national media attention, which ratcheted up the pressure.

But Lucy and the candy factory remain the operative metaphor. In North Carolina, as of this writing, GOP lawmakers were busily searching for new ways to push forward with voter ID requirements. In Texas, legislators came back with a version of the law that allowed people without an ID to vote, as long as they sign a sworn affidavit giving a good reason for not having ID in the first place—which is better, but voting rights advocates still fear that this sort of cumbersome procedure, which carries the threat of criminal penalties for falsification, might intimidate the well intentioned from even attempting the process. Nevertheless, in early 2018, the courts upheld this version. And in Kansas, officials continue to try to implement a measure requiring proof of citizenship to register, even though proponents' efforts to "prove" hordes of noncitizens are trying to vote have repeatedly gone down in flames in the courts.

How Bad Is It?

University of California legal scholar Richard L. Hasen, who obsessively tracks every skirmish in what he calls the "voting wars" for his indispensable Election Law Blog, has bluntly observed that we have seen the evolution of red-state election law and blue-state election law. And those voting wars have spread to the courts: The onslaught of such measures has led to a striking increase in legal battles over them as well. Hasen attempted to quantify this trend in a study, by tallying up what he called election-related litigation on the state and federal level over the past four decades. He concluded:

> In the period since 2000, the amount of election-related litigation has more than doubled compared to the period before 2000, from an average of 94 cases per year in the period just before 2000 to an average of 258 cases per year in the post-2000 period.
>
> Even compared to the 2012 presidential election cycle, litigation is up significantly; it was 23 percent higher in the 2015–2016 presidential election season than in the 2011–2012 presidential election season, and at the highest level since at least 2000 (and likely ever).[14]

By Hasen's count, there were substantially more such legal challenges during the 2015–2016 cycle than during any other two-year cycle leading into a presidential election since the lead-up to 2000. And this legal escalation, too, has been saturated with partisanship and polarization. As Republicans have intensified their efforts to pass laws restricting the ballot, a loose coalition of good-government and civil rights groups have increasingly challenged them in court—and they have often been allied with Democratic lawmakers, for the obvious reason (say it with me this time) that those rules are often designed to depress the vote among Democrat-aligned constituencies.

Even worse still, this partisan divide may also be seeping into the judiciary, mirroring the divergence of political realities among party elites and voters noted above. For instance, Hasen points out that in the North Carolina case, a worrisome pattern developed, in which Republican-appointed judges at the district court, appeals court, and Supreme Court level were significantly less troubled by the state's voter suppression provisions than were Democratic-appointed judges. When the Supreme Court invalidated the North Carolina law by letting an appeals court ruling against it stand, Chief Justice John Roberts—a conservative appointed by a Republican president, George W. Bush—went out of his way to issue a statement clarifying that this decision was based on procedural grounds and should *not* be taken as a ruling against the law on the legal merits—not exactly a strong rebuttal of a law considered profoundly discriminatory by the courts that had previously reviewed it.

The point is not that judges are actively gaming their rulings to favor the interests of the parties that appointed them. Rather, it's that judges are selected or blocked by parties in the first place because of their legal backgrounds, histories, and ideological worldviews—which color their judicial reactions to limits on voting. Hasen observes darkly that "the continued hyperpartisanship surrounding rules for conducting elections," combined with "increased litigation" over those rules, could enmesh the courts in "ever more difficult decisions" about these matters. If judicial decisions continue to "break down across party lines," Hasen concludes, this could undermine "respect for courts and the rule of law," as well as public confidence in the "legitimacy of the election system."[15]

As mentioned in the previous chapter, in 2016, Republican Senate majority leader Mitch McConnell refused to give a hearing to former president Barack Obama's nominee to fill the Supreme Court seat of the deceased Antonin Scalia. This refusal was itself a dramatic partisan perversion of norms—and because of the move, that seat has since been filled by President Trump's nominee, the very conservative Neil Gorsuch. With that appointment, and the retirement of Justice Anthony Kennedy in June 2018, the court is further tilting against placing discernible limits on future voter suppression tactics, even if those tactics get worse (a topic this book will discuss later). Think of it as a kind of partisan double whammy: It isn't just that our election rules are more captive to partisan motives than at any time in recent history. It's also that the institution that might provide a check on excessive partisan rigging of the voting rules—the judiciary—could prove increasingly divided along partisan lines on these matters, all the way to the top. Which means this deep schism over the most fundamental aspects of how to conduct political competition may grow ever more bitter and acrimonious—a subject we will turn to next.

3

Demographic Destiny: The Battle to Shape the Electorate

Donald Trump is probably the only candidate in all of U.S. history who campaigned explicitly and unabashedly on the notion that the outcome produced by our electoral system would be legitimate only if he won. At one point in the fall of 2016, Trump was asked point-blank if he'd accept the legitimacy of the results if rival Hillary Clinton prevailed, and he declined to say. ("I will keep you in suspense," he replied.[1]) After taking some criticism for the dodge, Trump strode forth before a roaring rally crowd in Ohio and doubled down in remarkable fashion. "I would like to promise and pledge to all of my voters and supporters and to all of the people of the United States that I will totally accept the results of this great and historic presidential election," he shouted. Then, after a dramatic pause: "*If I win.*"[2]

This striking display from Trump, who was at the time trailing in polls, was nothing less than an effort to delegitimize a loss—in advance. Presidential historians groped for precedents and found none. Throughout the 2016 campaign, Trump repeatedly cast doubt on the integrity of our political system. He cast the whole U.S. electoral apparatus as "rigged." He called on his supporters to monitor the polls in "certain areas" where "bad things happen."[3] In another effort at this less-than-subtle racial messaging, he railed at rallies in Pennsylvania that the election was going to be "stolen," in one case citing unspecified "reports" he had heard about "Philadelphia." He said: "Everybody knows what I'm talking about."[4] And indeed, everyone *did* know what he was talking about: Nonwhite urban dwellers who would allegedly steal the election from the white working-class folk who populated the state's industrial and rural heartland—the Real America for which Trump purported to speak.

At times, Trump elaborated on his conspiracy mongering in cartoonishly grotesque ways. He accused unnamed border security officials of letting undocumented immigrants "pour into the country so they can go and vote."[5] Even after the election, Trump continued to claim the voting totals were illegitimate—despite having been elected president—and that he would have won the popular vote (which he lost by nearly three million) if not for massive voter fraud.[6]

Whether by instinct or through careful study—the former is the more likely—Trump knew his audience. He grasped that large swaths of Republican voters could be counted on to believe these types of claims, and so they did. In the fall of 2016, polls showed that two thirds of Republican voters saw voter fraud as a more serious problem than voter disenfranchisement, while only 37 percent of Americans overall held that position.[7] As Trump recognized, Republican voters were already inclined to believe these things, because Republican elected officials have been sounding the alarm about voter fraud—and wielding the specter of stolen elections to energize their voters and justify strict limits on voting—for many years. Trump merely took these types of assertions and inflated them in unprecedentedly garish, outsize, and hallucinatory ways. Indeed, underscoring the point, while some Republican lawmakers did condemn Trump's most over-the-top claims, many GOP officials lent careful rhetorical support to the general thrust of Trump's warning of election rigging and fraudulent voting, while taking pains to do so in more reasonable-sounding tones. They, too, knew Republican voters would eagerly accept the story Trump was telling. The polarization around voting rules described in the last chapter is not simply a matter of elites in each party trying to game the field for partisan advantage. The divisions on these matters actually reach deep into the two parties' electorates.

Why Republicans Are Obsessed with Voter Fraud

In some parts of North Carolina—the site of some of the most pitched battles over voting rights we've seen in recent years—the locals still feel a special attachment to reruns of

The Andy Griffith Show. This hit 1960s situation comedy, which offered a nostalgic picture of a bygone era of small-town America, was set in a fictional North Carolina community known as Mayberry, where Andy Taylor, played by Griffith, served as the warm, wise sheriff. On the show, the characters sometimes enthused about a big nearby town known as Siler City—a real place in central North Carolina that at the time boasted a population of over 4,000 people. The actress who played Aunt Bee, Andy's aunt, even retired to Siler City, where she later died in 1989 at the age of eighty-six.

One day in 2016, Douglas Heye, a young, personable Republican consultant who grew up around an hour from Siler City but had never visited it (despite watching the show throughout his childhood), drove over on a whim to have a look. Heye was surprised to discover a profusion of Hispanic-owned businesses in the center of town. "This was your stereotypical North Carolina town," Heye told me. For him, this captured the slow transformation of small cities throughout the country at the hands of arriving Latino immigrants. He told me this story as a way to illustrate, in a tongue-in-cheek way, the surprise that many Republican lawmakers have experienced as they have awakened to the presence of nonwhite voters in their communities—and the long-term demographic challenges that loom for the Republican Party if it does not improve its appeal to them.

Heye—who worked on Capitol Hill for years as an aide to the House GOP leadership and is now an independent consultant and frequent guest on political chat shows—has long been puzzled by his party's general response to this demographic shift. He frequently talks to GOP candidates and lawmakers, urging them to appreciate their party's need to improve its appeal to nonwhites. One topic that sometimes comes up in these conversations is voting rights. Heye has argued to his listeners that onerous restrictions on voting will be inevitably perceived as efforts to disenfranchise minorities, no matter how vociferously they defend them in the name of cracking down on alleged voter fraud. "Ultimately when so much of your focus is on restricting access to the ballot, requiring ID, and restricting access to ID, clearly there is an ulterior motive," Heye told me. "You have to know that it'll be perceived as racial bias."

It's not always easy, however, to say whether—or to what degree—the desire to suppress the votes of minorities in particular, as opposed to merely any constituencies who vote Democratic, really *is* the motive behind restrictions on voting. Advocates for voting rights have claimed for many years that these restrictive measures are, at bottom, about Republican lawmakers fighting a kind of rearguard action against demographic trends that are slowly but inexorably working against their party. But it is hard to definitively prove this charge to be systematically true. Certainly there are multiple individual instances in which the evidence explicitly suggests that a driving motive behind these measures is to suppress the votes of Democratically aligned nonwhite constituencies (such as in the case of the North Carolina voting law that was blocked by the courts[8]). And when I asked Heye whether his general sense, having worked with numerous GOP lawmakers, is whether they view voting restrictions as a racially conscious means to slow the impact of ongoing demographic transformation, Heye replied carefully. "I don't know that that's happening," he said in a tone of mock innocence, before adding: "But I *know* that that's happening."

As the Democratic Party has grown more diverse in recent years, it was inevitable that voter suppression tactics would take on an increasingly racial cast. As noted, the voting wars of this era really got going after the bitterly contested Florida recount in the 2000 presidential election focused operatives in both parties on the impact of voting rules on small but potentially decisive margins of turnout. Thus, the Justice Department under George W. Bush reoriented its focus toward crackdowns on alleged voter fraud, rather than toward its traditional enforcement of voting rights, a huge shift in priorities.[9] Concurrently, states began increasingly implementing limits on voting. But it was Obama's 2008 candidacy, powered by an electorate of unprecedented racial diversity and the influx of new voters he had inspired, that really shined a light on the threat that demographic change posed to the GOP's long-term fortunes. (It's no accident that the 2008 election inspired the GOP's focus on voter fraud to take the form of an overheated and absurd obsession with the notion that a community organization known as ACORN was spearheading an elaborate plot to steal the election for Barack Obama. This claim—for which there was zero evidence—was echoed by none other than the Republican nominee for president, Arizona senator John McCain.[10]) Obama's victory, seeming to confirm that rising demographic threat—which then coincided with the massive GOP takeover of state legislatures in 2010—helped fuel a wave of new state-level initiatives limiting access to voting. Indeed, Rutgers University political scientist Lorraine Minnite has written that the relentless evocation of spectral voter fraud has become tantamount to a new southern strategy—that is, a new spin on Richard Nixon's concerted use of racial signaling to stoke white resentment and mobilization. As Minnite noted, partisan Republican voters have become "energized by the tarring of Democrats as cheaters," and the threat of mobilization of fraudulent voters furthers the "association of Democrats with a radicalized crime-prone underclass."[11]

Certainly someone can genuinely believe that voter fraud is a threat—and to support limits on voting as a result—without seeing this threat in racial terms. Still, it is undeniable that conspiratorial suggestions of voter fraud have frequently been riddled with race-baiting appeals. And Donald Trump, by spinning fantasies about enormous numbers of undocumented immigrants voting and by casting the voter fraud threat as one concentrated in urban centers, essentially made racial signaling as it applies to the voter fraud debate explicit.

Whit Ayres, one of the most prominent pollsters in the

Republican Party, offers his own unique glimpse into what is going on with Republican voters on these matters. Ayres told me that he believes voter fraud is a real problem in some cases, and argues that there is nothing wrong with voter ID laws if they are appropriately drawn to avoid disenfranchisement. But Ayres—a genial, patrician, gray-haired fellow who seems to hail from a bygone era of country-club Republicanism that has been thrown on the defensive by the forces Trump has unleashed within the party—has also spent years arguing that his party must do more to evolve along with what he described as "the long-term demographic trends that are changing this country."

"You can fight a rearguard action here and there, but you need to adapt your strategy toward a changing America," Ayres told me. He added that if Republicans continue trying to adopt measures designed to limit access to the ballot, such as early voting, it risks making it seem as if "you don't believe in your ideas and that we can't sell them to people who don't look like us."

But Ayres—who has spent many, many years probing the attitudes of GOP voters through polling and focus groups—also offered some insights that carry more broadly disturbing implications for the debate over voting access. His research has discerned a general assumption among many GOP voters that elections are already rigged against them, via a shady alliance between minority voters and the Democratic Party that goes well beyond voter fraud and includes what is in effect vote buying via government handouts. This belief inclines GOP voters to accept or even applaud efforts to rewrite the voting rules, even in cases where the goal is merely partisan advantage. Ayres characterized this mindset as follows: "These minorities are all on the take. They are getting government benefits. We don't have an even playing field. You can't expect us to beat all of those people who are in the tank for the other side. We can't win with those people because the other side has their hooks into them."

There is ample reason to believe that Ayres is on to something. When 2012 GOP presidential candidate Mitt Romney was famously recorded by a cell phone at a closed-door gathering of well-heeled donors as he derided the "47 percent" of Americans who are dependent on government handouts and thus vote Democratic, he neatly crystallized such sentiments. Romney claimed that this freeloading block of Americans—nearly half the country—were going to vote for President Barack Obama "no matter what," adding that there was no point in trying to persuade them to vote Republican.[12] Polls showed a large chunk of GOP voters viewed Romney's comments favorably.[13]

Trump did not emphasize one key aspect of Romney's argument—that Democratic voters are bought off by social spending. But if anything, Trump placed *more* emphasis on the idea that electoral outcomes are fundamentally rigged against Republicans. Whether it is through government handouts or through voter fraud, the basic story line is that Republicans, in the words of Ayres, "don't have an even playing field."

Why Republicans tend to believe this tale in all its renditions is beyond the scope of this book. For our purposes, the point is that this widespread conviction among Republican voters—that electoral outcomes are already unfairly rigged against them—has been carefully cultivated by GOP leaders (and GOP-aligned media outlets and celebrity radio hosts) for many years. It continues to provide fertile ground in which arguments for further restrictions on voting can take root. And if many voters in one of the two major political parties already believe that our electoral system is producing outcomes of questionable legitimacy, they will be more easily encouraged to accept what you might call "counter-rigging" measures of increasingly dubious intent, which makes the possibility of shared agreement on fair voting rules even harder to attain.

Polarization as a Story About Race

Pollsters and political scientists have documented a rise in ideological sorting and polarization among the electorate on a range of issues, as well as a rise of what is called negative partisanship, in which voters are increasingly motivated not by their own party's policies but by dislike of the other side. Some political scientists believe the 2016 presidential election—in which Trump prevailed because dislike of the other side prevented major defections among GOP voters and lawmakers despite his being widely viewed as unfit for the presidency—represented a particularly toxic display of this trend, and signals more to come.[14] These broad developments also help explain why the parties have focused more energy in recent years on mobilizing their voters, because there is less to be gained from focusing on the persuasion of swing voters, who appear to be in many ways a vanishing species. Thus the parties have increasingly focused on voting rules, because mobilization on the margins can sometimes make a critical difference without requiring a major effort to win swing voters via persuasion.

But there's another dimension to this polarization as well: It is deeply entangled with race. Emory University political scientist Alan Abramowitz undertook an exhaustive study of the polarization of the electorate in recent decades and concluded that it has been heavily driven by what he calls a "racial realignment." This is the result of a confluence of factors—the increasing drift of white voters into the GOP; the growing racial diversity of the electorate since the 1980s, due to large-scale immigration and racial disparities in fertility rates; and the fact that the vast majority of the new nonwhite voters entering the electorate have identified with the Democratic Party. As Abramowitz summarized:

> Between 1992 and 2012, the nonwhite share of voters in presidential elections more than doubled, going from 13 percent to 28 percent. However, this growing racial and ethnic diversity had very different effects

on the two major parties. The nonwhite share of Republican voters increased modestly between 1992 and 2004, going from 4 percent to 12 percent, mainly due to Republican candidates' ability to attract a sizeable chunk of the growing Hispanic vote. After 2004, however, the nonwhite share of Republican voters fell to 10 percent in both 2008 and 2012, while the nonwhite share of Democratic voters increased steadily—from 21 percent in 1992 to 45 percent in 2012.[15]

That racial breakdown was roughly the same in 2016 and is likely to grow more pronounced over time, Abramowitz concluded. It is not hard to imagine what this might mean for the voting wars in future years. If those struggles get more and more intense, whether deliberate or not, efforts to limit voting by Democratic constituencies could increasingly target nonwhite constituencies, deepening the cycle of bitterness and anger. To recap the warning delivered above by GOP pollster Whit Ayres, it will increasingly look as if Republicans want to limit voting because they have concluded they can't sell their ideas "to people who don't look like us."

Voter Fraud Is Itself a Fraud

How new is all this? Throughout our history, allegations of fraudulent voting have been intimately tied up with efforts to restrict the vote for the purposes of influencing the partisan—and at times ethnic—makeup of the electorate.

In the early and mid-nineteenth century, some reformers began pushing voter registration systems that were justified in part as a measure to reduce fraud, but—according to their opponents—were actually designed to reduce political participation by poor people and immigrants, who, it was claimed, were voting illegally. Those measures were sometimes designed to reduce the opposition's electoral strength. At the end of that century, progressive elites associated reform with tighter regulation of voting that, while designed to reduce corruption and fraud and break the power of urban political machines, also restricted access for the poor and working class.

But the voter fraud that is often alleged today has little in common with the sort of corruption that existed throughout the nineteenth century. That species of fraud lives on in the popular mind via images such as that of New York's Boss Tweed clutching a cigar as he boasted about his control over the vote counting process, or of Tammany Hall operatives throwing ballot boxes into the East River. But these days, when political scientists and voting rights advocates—and, of course, proponents of ballot restrictions—use the term *voter fraud,* they are referring to a different kind of fraud: voter *impersonation* fraud. This occurs when an individual represents himself to be another person at the ballot box—either someone who appears on the voter rolls or has registered under a false name—and thus casts an illegitimate ballot. It is distinct from other types of contemporary fraud, such as registration fraud, in which people fake the registration of people to collect money for fulfilling voter registration drives, or absentee ballot fraud, which tends to involve the outright buying of mail-in votes. Both of those are real problems (though also rare). But impersonation fraud is the "problem" that stricter voter ID laws are meant to "solve."

Time and again over recent decades, academics and government officials have set out to find the widespread voter fraud that Republicans constantly alleged to be taking place. They have come up largely empty. The Bush administration's Justice Department spent five years trying to crack down on voter fraud—a major shift in priorities, as noted earlier—yet by 2007, the effort had turned up virtually no organized voter fraud.[16] There were a very small number of convictions, but those charged had mostly made mistakes on registration forms or misunderstood eligibility rules (which, again, are not the type of fraudulent in-person voting that Republicans have widely warned about to justify voter ID laws). Other attempts to discern voter fraud also came up empty. In 2007, Justin Levitt, a voting law expert at Loyola University, undertook an extensive review of recent elections that had been carefully scrutinized for voter fraud, and found that it was virtually nonexistent. He concluded: "It is more likely that an individual will be struck by lightning than that he will impersonate another voter at the polls."[17] Levitt revisited the question recently, by collecting as many incidents of voter fraud as he could find in primary, general, special, and municipal elections held across the country from 2000 to 2016. He has discovered only a few dozen incidents of voter fraud out of more than *one billion ballots* cast.[18]

When I spoke with him, Levitt joked he had revised his original 2007 conclusion that voter fraud is as infrequent as lightning strikes. "If anything, with rapid climate change, lightning strikes may be becoming more frequent, but voter fraud really isn't," he said.

More recently still, after the 2016 election—which Trump loudly claimed would be hijacked by undocumented immigrants and fraudulent voters—Philip Bump of *The Washington Post* conducted an exhaustive search of media sources and produced only four documented cases of voter fraud out of 135 million votes cast in the election.[19] As Trump continued to assert that there had been widespread fraud and illegal voting, a trio of academics in government and social science from Dartmouth College conducted an extensive study of county-level voting data in the 2016 election to test his claims. "We have found no evidence that could support anything like Trump's accusations," they concluded. "Voter fraud concerns fomented by the Trump campaign are not grounded in any observable features of the 2016 presidential election."[20]

In at least one case, the evidence *against* the prevalence

of voter fraud was so overwhelming that it helped change the mind of one of the most prominent conservative judges in the country. Richard Posner, who was appointed to the bench by Ronald Reagan in 1981, wrote a seminal opinion that upheld the Indiana voter ID law in 2007. But then, in a 2013 book, he conceded that voter fraud had come to be seen as "a means of voter suppression rather than fraud prevention."[21] And in 2014, as an appeals court judge, he completed his conversion, writing a withering dissent in a case involving the Wisconsin voter ID law discussed in the last chapter. In that dissent, Posner argued flatly that voter fraud is "essentially nonexistent in Wisconsin." But that's not all: Devastatingly, this conservative Reagan appointee who had famously upheld voter ID in the past also approvingly cited evidence in his dissent that such laws are both overwhelmingly the partisan handiwork of Republicans and are often explicitly designed to disenfranchise minorities.

The argument is not that voter fraud never happens. Rather, it's that it is exceedingly rare. And for good reason: It's a dumb way to try to influence an election. The penalty for voter fraud is harsh in most states, and under federal law, those convicted of it face up to five years in prison and a fine of as much as $10,000. Why risk that punishment to gain a single vote or a handful of votes for any given candidate? That said, it is challenging to completely dispel the myth of voter fraud, because it's pretty much impossible to reach *totally comprehensive and definitive* conclusions about its frequency. As Levitt told me: "To really get a for-sure comprehensive answer, you'd have to do a multiyear forensic analysis on every election in the country, in tens of thousands of tiny jurisdictions." He added: "Instead, responsible analysts rely on two different things: the totality of multiple limited studies (all of which seem to point in the same direction), and the absence of reliable studies to the contrary."

Maybe the best explanation for the lack of widespread instances of voter fraud is that there's very little voter fraud.

How Real Is the Threat of Disenfranchisement?

Just as academics have spent years trying to gauge how widespread a problem voter fraud really is, so, too, have academics spent years trying to gauge whether voter ID laws disenfranchise people. And on this front, the totality of the evidence is a good deal less definitive—in either direction.

New York University's Samuel Issacharoff looked at a number of studies of this question and reached several conclusions. First, many such studies have shown that minorities *are* less likely to possess the right kinds of identification at the outset. Thus it's reasonable to assume that such laws put them *at greater risk* of disenfranchisement. However, a number of studies have also turned up little discernible *impact* of such laws on the turnout of minorities, or on their turnout relative to other voter groups. What's more, during litigation against voter ID laws, opponents have produced relatively few examples of people who have suffered direct disenfranchisement by those laws.

But Issacharoff also noted that there are serious methodological difficulties involved in judging the ongoing impact of such laws in any kind of systematic way. For instance, one problem in assessing the impact of these laws on African American turnout in recent presidential elections is that Barack Obama was on the ballot in 2008 and 2012, and his galvanizing impact may have supplanted any dampening effect that might have otherwise shown up—and could still show up in the future. Another problem is that the strictest voter ID laws are quite recent, meaning that there has not been enough time to test their impact "against normal fluctuations in turnout," as Issacharoff puts it.[22]

Still, the evidence out there—which does show specific and glaring examples of disenfranchisement—does, in fact, present a strong indictment of such laws. After the 2016 presidential election, researchers conducted a survey of registered voters in Milwaukee and Dane counties in Wisconsin—two heavily African American Democratic strongholds—who did not cast a ballot. They found that 11 percent of these voters reported that they had not voted because under the state's voter ID law, they didn't have the required forms of identification. The study's authors calculated that this probably represented around 13,000 voters in those counties, but could have been as many as 23,000. An election official in Wisconsin told Ari Berman of *Mother Jones* magazine that it was "very probable" that due to voter suppression, "enough people were prevented from voting to have changed the outcome of the presidential election in Wisconsin."[23]

Similarly, a study by the Government Accountability Office, a nonpartisan, independent agency that produces research for Congress, found that changes to voter ID laws in Kansas and Tennessee likely produced a drop in turnout by two to three percentage points from the 2008 to the 2012 election, relative to states that didn't change their laws, with larger drops among young, African American, and newly registered voters.

In short, the evidence is mixed on how widespread the impact of voter ID laws really is in practice. But we can certainly say there is strong evidence that it does suppress untold numbers of votes.

Are We Seeing Another Backslide in Voting Access?

Obviously, it would be absurd to argue that what we are seeing now comes anywhere close to rivaling some of the biggest contractions in voting access that we've seen in U.S. history, such as the one inflicted on African Americans at the end of the nineteenth century. The question, though, is whether the current trend can actually be described as the beginnings of a meaningful contraction all the same. I put this question to a handful of voting rights historians and political scientists, and got a mix of responses that added up to one overall answer: It's too soon to tell, but it is a cause for genuine, legitimate worry, and demands vigilance.

One of those who are concerned about this possibility is the previously mentioned Alexander Keyssar. In his wonderfully detailed and sweeping history of the battles over the right to vote, the Harvard historian sounded a somewhat pessimistic tone about the contemporary voting wars. He noted that the twenty-first century is once again seeing a "narrowing of the portals to the ballot box" in "parts of the nation." When I asked him if he thought this narrowing represented the beginnings of a contraction in voting access similar to previous ones in our history, he replied that it's a hard thing to measure and a bit too soon to gauge the impact of some of the stricter new voting rules. He added, "It's an alarm worth sounding—while finding the right decibel level so as not to sound too alarmist." Nathaniel Persily, a professor at Stanford Law School who is one of the foremost experts in the country on the arcana of voting laws and rules, echoed Keyssar's sense of things. "The jury is still out on how big an impact any of these changes have actually had," he told me. Persily noted that it is "fair to say that some contemporary political actors intend to contract voting access for partisan reasons," by which he meant that an overall contraction is their goal. But he added: "It remains an open question whether they are succeeding and to what degree." In other words, they *might* succeed.

Election Law Blog's Richard Hasen is somewhat more pessimistic. He emailed:

> We have already entered into a period of contraction of voting rights. In many states, it is harder to vote now than it was 5 years ago. We need to stop thinking of our progress on voting rights as moving only in the direction of greater enfranchisement. At this moment in time, things are moving in the wrong direction. While it is hard to quantify how much these laws are deterring voting, they are certainly deterring some (and more and more as these laws get stricter). What's worse, they are curtailing access for no good reason.

This seems like the appropriate posture: Many states are increasingly passing laws *designed* to make it harder to vote, which itself represents a backslide of sorts. And while it's hard to measure in the moment how much this will limit ballot access, there is no reasonable justification for many of these *efforts* to limit that access, particularly the ones that appear deliberately designed to do so with an eye toward manipulating the makeup of the electorate.

We have no way of knowing how much worse the targeted Republican efforts to discourage voting will get. But the deeper unknown is even more troubling: We don't know what will happen over time if larger numbers of Americans—whether it's Republicans who grow ever more panicked about the phantom threat of voter fraud, or Democrats who witness ever more tactics designed to suppress their votes—operate from the premise that our political system is regularly at risk of producing illegitimate outcomes. As we'll see in the pages to come, that erosion of faith presents a danger that goes well beyond the voting booth.

4

"This Dystopia Where Nothing Is True . . . and Chaos Reigns": The Struggle to Get More Americans to Vote

In early December 2017, many liberals and Democrats were in a state of high anxiety and deep despair. It looked as if an open bigot with a history of lawlessness and alleged pedophilia might win a seat in the U.S. Senate with the backing of President Trump, whose agenda he had vowed to champion. Republican Roy Moore had a history of revolting anti-gay and anti-Muslim remarks,[1] and had twice been removed from the judicial bench in Alabama for placing God's law above human law—first by defying a federal court that ordered him to remove a marble statue of the Ten Commandments from the state judicial building, and second by flouting the U.S. Supreme Court's recent ruling that established a constitutional right to gay marriage.[2] Now, running for Senate, the candidate had been hit by explosive allegations from a series of seemingly credible women who claimed he had made sexual advances on them when they were in their teens.[3] Yet Moore had denied the charges and appeared to still have a reasonable chance of victory, due to Alabama's deep red hue—in 2016, Trump had carried the state by 28 points.

Moore beat back the charges of unwanted sexual advances by casting them as evidence of a liberal media conspiracy against conservative Christians. His allies had tried to bait reporters into covering fake allegations against Moore in hopes of discrediting the careful media reporting that had brought the real allegations to light. Trump himself publicly suggested that Moore's denials should be believed, and his aides let it be known that the president saw in the abuse stories the same kind of media vilification that he, Trump, had endured in the coverage of women who had accused him of unwanted advances. Adding to the anxiety, Alabama has a strict voter ID law, leading many liberals and Democrats to fret that a close race could be tipped to Moore if enough African Americans in the state were blocked from voting. In this nightmare scenario, a Republican win would show that bigotry, lawlessness, and allegations of sexual predation could be rendered nonfactors by a combination of voter suppression and full-blown efforts to discredit careful fact-based media inquiry, amounting to a kind of triumph of Trumpist degradation of our political system.

It's worth asking how someone like Moore could possibly be elected to the U.S. Senate given all of his horrible baggage. One important reason was that not enough people vote. Moore was not the choice of establishment Republicans. He had prevailed in a primary over a more conventional Republican in part because only around 15 percent of eligible GOP voters at most had cast a ballot.[4] While Moore's history and temperament—especially in contrast with those of his Democratic opponent, former prosecutor Doug Jones—made the race much closer than Alabama's Republican lean suggested it should be, the only conceivable way the Democrat could win is if his voters turned out at outsize rates. And the Alabama secretary of state was predicting a lackluster turnout of around 25 percent of eligible voters—which might have been devastating to Jones's chances.

If you are a political operative or even just an engaged political observer, you know that it can be an exhilarating feeling when election returns are coming in and the tallies demonstrate in real time that your candidate's voters are turning out in great numbers. At the same time, it can be deeply dispiriting when your side's voters are staying home. I recall being in touch on election day in 2014 with a Democratic operative involved in the North Carolina Senate race of that year. This operative dejectedly told me late into the night that he realized the Democrat was going to lose, because the votes just kept coming in from the state's deep red counties, while Democratic voters just weren't materializing in great enough numbers to counter them. As he lamented: "We've run out of bodies." Indeed, it was a year in which Republicans routed Democratic candidates in midterm elections everywhere, due in part to lackluster Democratic turnout.

Fortunately, Alabama's secretary of state was wrong. More than 1.3 million of Alabama's 3.3 million voters turned out, in a showing of just over 40 percent.[5] As a result, Jones narrowly prevailed by less than two points, in part because that higher turnout was driven by larger-than-expected showings in Democratic strongholds, including heavily African American ones. Internal Democratic polling had registered that their voters were unexpectedly energized and had come to view the race as "more important" than most political contests. If the threat of voter suppression ever had any chance of tipping the race to Moore, it was overwhelmed by a mobilized electorate.

To be sure, the turnout of 40 percent in the Alabama Senate race wasn't exactly something to celebrate, since it meant that a depressingly large number of voters in the state simply didn't participate. But what the results showed is that while low voter participation sometimes has the potential to fuel very bad political outcomes, relatively higher participation sometimes has the capacity to avert them. While it was unfortunate that it required a candidate as self-evidently awful as Roy Moore to make it possible, Jones's win shattered recent trends: he was the first Democrat to win a Senate seat in Alabama in twenty-five years, overcoming the deep structural advantages that Democrats have faced in southern states that have trended increasingly red.

Lots and Lots of Americans Don't Vote

Two political scientists—Benjamin Page and Martin Gilens, professors at Northwestern and Princeton Universities—recently summarized the gravity of the deficit in voting with clarity and vividness:

> In today's U.S. presidential elections—big national spectacles, where the stakes are very high—some media pundits sound pleased when just 65 percent or so of eligible citizens cast ballots. The figure is often closer to 60 percent, and in 2016 it was only about 59 percent. That is, in the most important elections we hold, more than *one-third* of eligible Americans *do not vote*. U.S. turnout rates are lower than those of many other countries, including such developing nations as Nicaragua, Sri Lanka, and Ghana. We ranked number thirty-one in turnout among the seventy-six countries that held presidential elections between 2004 and 2014.
>
> Turnout is even lower in "off-year" elections for the U.S. Congress, when no presidential candidates are around to generate media coverage and focus people's attention. In nonpresidential years, only about 40 percent of eligible Americans vote. This rate is far lower than the typical turnout for parliamentary elections in other countries. Off-year turnout in the United States ranks near the bottom for parliamentary elections around the world, among poor countries as well as

rich ones. Between 2004 and 2014, we came in nearly dead last: *113th* out of 114 countries.[6]

Still, it's worth asking why so many activists and political scientists believe low voter participation and engagement is actually a problem to begin with. For one thing, as the example of Alabama showed, it can help boost the prospects of extremist candidates. (This doesn't mean higher turnout guarantees the defeat of extremist candidates, but low-turnout elections do sometimes help them. For instance, in the 2018 Virginia Republican gubernatorial primary, Corey Stewart, a candidate with a history of palling around with white supremacists, won the nomination over a former Green Beret who was backed by the party establishment, thanks in part to lower turnout.) And low participation can produce "undemocratic" outcomes if, generally speaking, the voters who do participate prove unrepresentative of the American people, or even of the makeup of a higher-turnout electorate. Careful research has shown that this correlation often does exist. Jan Leighley and Jonathan Nagler, political scientists at American and New York Universities, recently undertook an exhaustive study of the socioeconomics of voter turnout in several decades of presidential elections leading up to 2008. They found that while there have been some success stories—turnout among women and African Americans has risen disproportionately over that period—generally speaking, highly educated and wealthier voters have consistently turned out at far greater rates than less educated and poorer voters have. Turnout among Latino voters has also consistently been low, relative to that among non-Hispanic whites. This has meant that the voting electorate has not been demographically representative. And that could also have ideological implications: Leighley and Nagler concluded that on economic issues in particular, there has been "consistent overrepresentation of conservative views among voters compared to nonvoters."[7]

That problem is itself a worthwhile reason to favor efforts to boost voter turnout and mobilization, particularly among relatively marginalized groups. But for our purposes here, there's another reason to aspire to that goal: more voter participation and engagement could offer a partial solution to some of the maladies that are currently ailing our democracy.

Barack Obama's Warning

In December 2017, Barack Obama angered many Republicans by delivering a speech in which he seemed to compare the current moment to the period before the rise of Nazi Germany. "You have to tend to this garden of democracy, otherwise things can fall apart fairly quickly," he warned in a speech to the Economic Club of Chicago. "And we've seen societies where that happens." Obama invited his crowd of well-heeled listeners to imagine that their gathering was akin to a scene one might have seen in Europe between the wars, a ballroom "in Vienna in the late 1920s or 1930s that looked pretty sophisticated, and seemed as if, with the music and art and literature and science that was emerging, would continue into perpetuity. And then 60 million people died. An entire world was plunged into chaos. So you've got to pay attention—and vote."[8]

Conservatives immediately pounced on the remarks, with some disingenuously suggesting that Obama had compared Trump to Hitler, and others claiming, with some justification, that the historical parallel was flawed. But the much more interesting and significant thing that Obama said in that speech was his assertion that the way to keep democracy healthy and vibrant was to *pay attention and vote*—in other words, that the real threat to democracy is complacency about its durability, and that the antidote to democratic deterioration is engagement. In this telling, democratic backsliding can take place when too many voters are looking the other way.

In private remarks to party officials and donors, Obama has expanded a bit on this argument. Ever since leaving office, he has been raising money for specific Democratic candidates, as well as for something called the National Democratic Redistricting Committee, which promotes Democratic candidates for state legislatures across the country, with the express purpose of winning back more power over the drawing of state legislative and House maps. This could increase the Democratic Party's representation in the

House, as will be discussed later. But this needn't be seen solely as a partisan goal: If the maps that result are actually *more fair*, as opposed to simply *better for Democrats*, on a macro level that would generally improve our democracy. In Obama's view, central to accomplishing both those goals has been an insistence on boosting voting. For instance, Obama made this case at a fundraiser for Democratic candidates at the New York City home of a retired financier in November 2017. According to a person who was present at the event, Obama told his listeners: "Our entire focus has to be on . . . activating people, not just in a few places, but across the country." This, he added, could "change the mood and reverse the narrative that somehow we are moving into this dystopia where nothing is true, and we just rage at each other, and the government can't function, and chaos reigns."[9]

It says a great deal about the state of our politics that it seems impossible that a politician might care about our system's overall functioning—in addition to caring about his own and his party's fortunes. But believe it or not, those two things can coexist. Yes, Obama wants to help elect more Democrats. But he also believes that more political engagement and participation may serve as an antidote to disillusionment with our current political moment—as an answer to the deep sense that many Americans have that the Trump era is debasing our politics to the point where the possibility of political discourse based on shared facts is dissolving beneath our feet.

By saying this, Obama touched on a point much discussed not only by candidates and political operatives but in a wide range of scholarly literature. The core question is whether more democratic participation has inherent value, both for the participants and for the health of our politics. As it turns out, answering that question is harder than it seems.

"More Democracy" Versus the "Realists"

Close observers have long been divided over some of the most fundamental questions at the heart of what ails democracy and what can be done to improve it. Some believe that the answer to improving democracy is "more democracy," while others take a much more skeptical view of that proposition.

Perhaps the most forceful statement of the skeptics in recent years is a groundbreaking work by political scientists Christopher Achen and Larry Bartels called *Democracy for Realists*. Their book offers a bracingly disenchanted account of how they believe democracy really works and what truly motivates voters. Achen and Bartels argue that most of us are in the grip of what they call the "folk theory of democracy," in which we have an overly rosy view of the deliberations of the democratic citizen. Most voters, they conclude, are woefully ill informed about politics and are not genuinely motivated by issues in any case. Instead, their political choices are mostly motivated by a sense of social and partisan identity. They choose their candidates based on a complicated process of identification, in which they sense that those candidates belong to the same social and political groups that they do. Voters then work backward from that point, persuading themselves that they support their candidates' positions in order to rationalize that predetermined identity-based choice. As a result of this circularity, when candidates and parties articulate their positions on issues, they are mostly furnishing voters with rationalizations designed to pull them more firmly into the fold of their social and political group, into which they were already inclined to drift anyway.

Thus, Achen and Bartels claim, efforts to make our politics "more democratic" by putting voters in direct control of policy outcomes—such as initiatives and referenda—have often produced bad outcomes. The real route to improving democracy, in their telling, is to accept that in the real world, policy decisions are often made by elites, and these decisions don't reflect actual voter preferences in any meaningful sense. Yes, once they are elected, officials have to be responsive to voters and popular impulses, but in this model, voters hold elected officials accountable retrospectively, by assessing the fruits of their overall performance, rather than by evaluating their ongoing policy choices. And that process of retrospective evaluation is itself deeply flawed; ordinary voters sometimes irrationally give officials credit for positive outcomes during their tenures (and blame them for negative ones) that those officials aren't responsible for producing. By this account, more voting, or "more democracy," will not automatically produce improved government; the better course is to build elite coalitions of politicians and interest groups more likely to intelligently govern in the public interest. These will ultimately produce more genuinely responsive government than will politicians who—even if popularly elected—are captured by a different set of self-interested elites such as wealthy special interests, whose dominance over the process should be combated through reform. The role of voters in this process is complicated—realistically, it's often hard to say just how much influence they really have—and the prospects for improving democratic citizenship within this framework are challenging and to some degree uncertain.[10]

The "more democracy" school of thought, by contrast, finds this skepticism to be less compelling or worrisome, or at least to be somewhat misplaced. Political scientists in this camp generally believe that the way to improve our politics is to make it more democratic wherever possible. This entails removing barriers to voting to maximize participation and to bring nonvoters into the process, which theoretically will make elected leaders more accountable to a broader electorate. Political scientists who subscribe to this view do not find it persuasive when critics point out that voters are often deeply uninformed about issues or are motivated to vote by factors such as group identity. They believe that while individual voters often are woefully uninformed, this tells only part of the story: large groups of voters, they argue, often *do* collectively arrive, albeit somewhat belatedly, at policy judgments that are rational and prove stable over time. While voters often do take their cues on policy from elites, they also discuss these views with one another and arrive at a set of positions that, at least to some degree, reflect a real set of values and priorities.

This latter view was set out by the previously mentioned political scientists Benjamin Page and Martin Gilens in their 2017 book, *Democracy for America?* In it, they concluded that "Americans, as a collectivity, hold policy preferences that are generally real, stable, consistent, coherent, and reflective of the available information," and that ordinary citizens can ultimately be counted on to "correctly judge what the common good entails." Thus, removing barriers to participation can improve our politics in its own right.[11]

The purpose of this chapter is not to litigate this debate. I bring it up to illustrate that the question of how to improve democratic citizenship and our political culture is a profound and difficult one with no simple set of answers. Both of these frameworks have considerable value and explanatory power, and despite certain fundamental differences, both suggest that boosting participation should be a goal that we all strive for. Indeed, as even the realists Achen and Bartels point out, if poor people were more organized politically and if turnout was "higher and more equal"—that is, more representative—then "American government would function better." (After all, even in the realist framework, the worldviews and governing approaches of elites are at least to some degree beholden to voters.) They also point to scholarship that "suggests that democratic political engagement may indeed have important implications for civic competence and other virtues," and add that "participation in democratic processes may contribute to better citizenship" that can produce "self-reinforcing improvements in civic culture."

Other recent scholarship has underscored this point. One 2016 study found that when nonvoters are induced to vote in elections, they seek to inform themselves about those elections, which led the study's author to conclude that efforts to encourage participation "can lead to both a more informed population, and better quality electoral outcomes."[12]

It's Hard to Get More People to Vote

But guess what? Getting more people to participate is *really hard to do*. While many states have recently tried to make voting harder (as we have seen), the last four decades have also seen many states adopt various measures designed to make it easier to vote. These include measures permitting early voting, same-day and election-day registration, no-excuse-needed absentee voting (in which voters can request that a ballot is mailed to them without offering a reason they cannot get to the polls), and in a few cases, a vote-by-mail option for all voters in all elections. As of this writing, thirty-seven states allow a period of early voting, and seventeen states permit same-day registration. All fifty states allow certain voters to request a ballot by mail, but only twenty-seven of them will send ballots to voters who haven't explained why they need to vote that way. Only three have all-mail voting, in which ballots are mailed to all eligible voters in every election, with limited in-person voting options.[13]

Many of the states that have undertaken such reforms are red states, which illustrates (as we noted in earlier chapters) that it is overly simplistic to declare that all Republican officials uniformly want to make it harder to vote. We should also acknowledge that a good number of Republican election officials—many of whom are career administrators, as opposed to elected lawmakers—take their public duty to oversee elections very seriously and want them to run smoothly and inclusively for all voters. That said, these facts can coexist with the broader generalization that Republican lawmakers as a general rule undoubtedly *do* want to make it harder to vote, while Democratic lawmakers as a general rule want to make voting easier. Here's why: Innovations such as early voting are popular among red state voters who appreciate the convenience of it. Yet in many red states, efforts to make such measures available to voters across the board have coexisted with efforts to restrict the franchise (such as voter ID laws), which are in multiple cases (as we have seen) very targeted toward specific groups of voters who happen to vote Democratic. Thus, some states have implemented measures to make voting more convenient for *all* their voters, while putting in place other ones designed to make it harder for *certain groups of them* in a manner that entrenches the power of GOP lawmakers. What's more, as we have also seen, in some red states, GOP lawmakers have more recently attempted to cut, or have actually reduced, previously established periods of early voting, including specific ones that Democratic-leaning constituencies opt for, sometimes out of an express desire to help Republicans.

Still, while we know such measures do make voting easier, do they actually boost voter turnout in a way that improves our democracy? To employ what political scientists often refer to as the cost-benefit theory of voting, the idea is that reformers can boost participation by reducing the "cost" of participation—that is, the amount of effort required to vote. The Holy Grail of such efforts is to bring into the process more *non*voters, who (as noted above) often tend to be poorly educated.

Studies gauging the impact of early voting laws on turnout have offered mixed results. Two of the political scientists mentioned above—Jan Leighley and Jonathan Nagler—have found that early voting might have a better chance of boosting turnout if early voting periods were to be *dramatically* expanded beyond their typical lengths. But Leighley and Nagler also concluded that the early voting periods actually adopted by states may simply be shifting around the timing of voting of people who probably would have voted anyway, a finding supported by other scholarship. Leighley and Nagler did find evidence that states adopting election day registration sometimes see higher turnout on average—that's good—but that the impact has been comparable on both well-educated and poorly educated voters, meaning it doesn't necessarily bring in a larger proportion of the underrepresented latter, and thus doesn't necessarily make the electorate more representative.

Their overall conclusion was yes, reducing the "cost" of voting sometimes does mean more people vote on average, particularly where election day registration is concerned. But even in cases where efforts to boost turnout had some success, they may not have brought us much closer to the goal of bringing in larger percentages of poorly educated voters.[14]

To be clear, the fact that efforts to boost participation have been disappointing in no way suggests that efforts to restrict participation are not a big deal. As noted in earlier chapters, those measures *have* had a pernicious impact. And making it easier to vote has its own inherent virtues, which probably helps explain why voters like the policies that do that. It's just not clear how far these efforts take us in the direction of that Holy Grail: making our electorates more representative and improving our politics.

This One Reform Holds Real Promise

For all of that, one reform does hold out the promise of a serious boost to political participation that could move us toward more representative electorates: universal, automatic voter registration. Under this policy, people who are eligible to vote are generally registered to do so by government agencies with which they've conducted business—say, their state's department of motor vehicles—unless they explicitly decline. Those agencies transfer information about voters they have registered to their state's election officials. As of this writing, some twelve states have approved a system like this, and bills doing the same have been introduced in around twenty states during 2018.[15] So far, the only state that has conducted a presidential election using automatic voter registration is Oregon, in 2016. That measure automatically adds the name of any voting-age Oregonian who gives his or her information to the state Department of Motor Vehicles—and has confirmed citizenship—to the voter rolls, unless he or she opts out.

The early returns on the Oregon experiment in automatic voter registration are very encouraging. A study by the liberal Center for American Progress found that in the 2016 president election, more than 272,000 previously unregistered people were added to the voter rolls by the new system, and more than 98,000 of them—around 5 percent of the electorate's total of 2 million voters—were new voters in that election. But did this make the electorate *more representative* of the overall population? According to that study, the answer is very likely yes. Sifting through the data, the study calculated that more than 116,000 of those added to the rolls had not voted in any presidential election going back to 2008—meaning that they likely would not have registered any other way if they hadn't been registered automatically. And more than 40,000 of those folks actually ended up voting. Both of those groups (the registered and the actual voters) contained disproportionately higher percentages of young people, as well as higher percentages of people who lived in lower-education, racially diverse, or low- and middle-income areas, than the state's overall population, so automatic voter registration was likely responsible not just for expanding the state's electorate, but also for broadening it as well.[16]

Why would automatic voter registration succeed where other measures—such as early voting—have been somewhat disappointing? The core insight that might explain this is that generally speaking, we human beings are lousy at planning ahead.

This idea has been explored in a more advanced manner by Sam Wang, a researcher in neuroscience at Princeton University. In other advanced democracies, voters don't have to register beforehand in order to cast a ballot. In the United States, voters in most states have to do so in advance of election day. As Wang—who has also done extensive research on various problems afflicting our democracy, such as gerrymandering—points out, this means that voters are forced to anticipate that they will need to take a preliminary action (registering to vote) well in advance of the second action (casting a ballot) that was the whole point of performing the preliminary one. Even people who generally think they want to vote have a decent chance of failing to do this, Wang's brain research has indicated. By contrast, automatic voter registration flips this around: The only preliminary action one can commit is to *opt out* of getting registered to vote; if you don't opt out, you're automatically registered. This, Wang says, triggers the "power of the default option," meaning that the easier option is to allow oneself to be registered to vote. "Human beings, it turns out, don't like to think very hard," Wang points out, only somewhat puckishly. "If it's a reasonable option, we'll choose the default option."[17] This may sound less than flattering to us human beings, but it's actually pretty unremarkable once you realize that many people have very busy lives and are not all that tuned in to the daily news about politics, which (let's face it) can often be mind-numbingly frustrating and impenetrable to nonjunkies.

This basic tendency of human beings to choose the default option has been documented in other areas. For instance, studies have shown that people are more likely to opt in to retirement savings plans and to agree to donate their organs after death—generally considered socially good outcomes—if those are the default options. And it is entirely plausible that automatic voter registration may disproportionately lead to more voting among young, poorer, and less educated people. If people from these groups are less likely to register in advance for socioeconomic reasons, Wang argues, then there is a decent chance they'll get disproportionately eased into the process by the removal of this barrier. "Young people, in some ways their brains aren't done, so they're less likely to plan ahead, and poor people have a lot of logistical pressures," Wang says. "Automatic voter registration is likely to have disproportionate benefits among the young and the poor. It makes it easier for everyone to vote. But it just so happens that people who have more obstacles to voting will be helped more."[18]

Automatic voter registration could also have cascading effects by fundamentally changing how campaigns are run—in particular, by changing how campaigns deploy resources to mobilize voters. Jeremy Bird, the national field director of Obama's 2012 campaign, illustrates this point with some fascinating statistics. Bird notes that during the 2012 election, the Obama campaign contacted registered voters by knocking on their doors or calling them some 150 million times. In those conversations, the campaign urged people who were already registered to actually come to the polls. The campaign also registered 2.1 million new voters, but doing this required a massive 700,000 volunteer shifts in the ten states targeted by the campaign. If those 2.1 million voters were already registered, Bird points out, that would have allowed those 700,000 volunteer shifts to be redeployed toward getting registered voters to the polls. "To redistribute our resources toward people who are already registered, and to have those conversations be about when, where, why, and how to vote," Bird says, would fundamentally change "the way in which we can bring people into the process." [19] This would mean that automatic voter registration holds out the promise of bringing in more voters than, say, same-day registration, since under the latter, would-be voters' names aren't on registration lists well in advance of election day and can't be repeatedly and intensively targeted the way they can if they are automatically registered and are on such lists.

Some have held out hope that automatic voter registration could also help crack one of the biggest obstacles to boosting voter turnout: the fact that nonvoters are often mired in a social context that discourages participation. Bird says that in trying to register people to vote, his organizers constantly bumped up against the problem that people who were not registered, and had a history of not voting, were usually surrounded by other people—friends, family members—who also were not registered and did not have a history of voting. "We would go into places where turnout has historically been low," Bird recounts of the 2012 campaign, places where "socioeconomically, people are struggling with a lot of different things day to day, and voting has not been a priority." In these places, Bird continues, voting "is not a party that everybody is going to. It's not something people are talking about. It's not something people are pressuring each other to do. It's not a big part of their identity, culture, and family tradition. It was a huge organizational challenge we encountered in almost every battleground state." And once again, Bird notes, people in these communities were often poorer or younger or less educated than the norm.

Veteran Democratic pollster Celinda Lake, who is one of the most seasoned political strategists in the party, has also frequently encountered this problem—and has done extensive research on it. Lake has conducted numerous focus groups of nonvoters and voters alike over the years for various good-government organizations who wanted to understand why people don't vote. Lake told me that what came up in these focus groups again and again is that nonvoters live in a social context heavily populated by other nonvoters. She recalled one focus group of unmarried female nonvoters in which the moderator asked them if they would vote if they knew their friends and family were voting. Lake says one woman replied, "I don't know who your friends and family are, but mine don't vote." Lake recounted another focus group, this one of young male nonvoters, in which she asked participants how the people around them would react if they did vote. One replied that his peers would say, "Why would you let yourself be played by the man?" As Lake concluded: "Voters are surrounded by networks of voters. Nonvoters are surrounded by networks of nonvoters." And such nonvoters, Lake added, are "surrounded by a network of cynics" who have "little understanding of the process." That dynamic is very hard to crack.[20]

Donald Green and Alan Gerber, political science professors at Columbia and Yale Universities, conducted exhaustive on-the-ground studies of the effectiveness of voter mobilization tactics and determined that contacts with voters can be effective in getting them to the polls. But the rub of the matter, they concluded, is that to be effective, these contacts have to be repeated and must be personal—meaning direct person-to-person contact, as opposed to, say, emails or robocalls—in order to begin to create a social milieu around them that "urges their participation."[21] Because automatic voter registration gives organizers extensive lists of nonvoters well in advance, it makes this much more doable.

Getting People to Vote Is Not Easy or Cheap

But it's still *very, very hard*. As Green and Gerber conclude from their research, providing social inducements to get people to vote via repeated and personalized contacts from campaigns "is neither easy or cheap." Their studies of the effectiveness of particular get-out-the-vote campaigns revealed that, generally speaking, only small fractions of those voters who are repeatedly contacted actually do end up voting. Thus, while these tactics do bring additional nonvoters into the process, each additional vote ends up costing campaigns a surprising amount of money and volunteer time.[22] As noted above, automatic voter registration would very likely help in this regard by freeing up campaign resources that would otherwise go to registering these voters in the first place. But the bottom line is that seriously improving voter participation remains a complicated and intractable problem.

The long-term hope of political scientists and campaign operatives who are trying to improve the situation is that automatic voter registration will help in getting a kind of foot in the door, as it were, among nonvoters. This might slowly have contagious spillover effects. "If we can get them [voters] involved in the process, and get them to vote a second time, all of a sudden you've created habitual voters," Bird says. "If you create voters, you create a tradition, where their kids start to go with them to the ballot box. It starts to become a cultural change."[23]

Still, it should also be stressed that when it comes to automatic voter registration, it is *very* early days. We have seen it used only in a presidential election in one state. As of this writing, of the twelve other states that have passed automatic voter registration laws, around half a dozen were trying to implement it in time for the 2018 elections, according to the Brennan Center, which has tracked these efforts through news reports and interviews with elections officials in the relevant states.[24] We probably won't be able to begin to seriously assess these new laws until the 2020 presidential race. And even at that point we may know little, because it remains challenging to gauge the impact of such efforts until numerous elections have played out with them in place.

What's more, there is a very long way to go before this

reform gets implemented more broadly. During the 2016 campaign Hillary Clinton rolled out an ambitious proposal for automatic voter registration on the national level, but it attracted very little media attention. As of now, the list of states that have passed this reform includes none of the major swing states aside from Colorado.[25] As this book will detail in later chapters, the brutally difficult imperative Democrats face if they are going to implement this and other reforms is to win back more ground on the level of the states—not just for the health of their party, but in order to improve our democracy.

5

Disinformation Nation

Donald Trump was a college student who had just begun to learn the family real estate business at the knee of his father when Hannah Arendt's 1967 essay "Truth and Politics" appeared in *The New Yorker* magazine. Almost exactly a half century later, now that Trump is president, Arendt's classic meditation has taken on new relevance, as a kind of touchstone to help us make sense of his own tortured relationship with the truth and what it says about the current state of our politics and democracy.

In that essay, Arendt, one of the great political theorists of the twentieth century, reflected at length on the relationship between power and factual truth. Factual truth—which she described as the depiction of facts and events—is fragile in the context of politics because it is "always in danger of being maneuvered out of the world" by the constant trafficking in falsehoods resorted to by politicians seeking to maintain power. This, Arendt suggested, puts factual truth and politics in perpetual antagonism. As a result, the preservation of the former depends on institutions that are theoretically supposed to be insulated from politics, and thus retain their independence, such as journalism. But, Arendt suggested, we can never rest assured that factual truth is safe, for one can always "imagine what the fate of factual truth would be" if power ends up "having the last say in these matters."[1]

Arendt's worldview, of course, was forged amid the twentieth-century European totalitarianism that was her primary topic. But here in Trump's America, the relationship between truth and politics has come under extraordinary strain, due to a toxic combination of factors—fake news, bot invasions, and unprecedented levels of lying and attacks on the press from the president himself—and a number of scholars and theorists have returned to Arendt in the quest to offer an account of it.

While Arendt's essay was published before Trump received his BA, it remains a profoundly useful lens through which to view his titanic BS—and the technological changes compounding the spread of BS and lies in so many other ways. As Columbia University media scholar Michael Schudson has explained, Arendt's treatise is an ideal starting point for making sense of the Trump era, with its confluence of Trump's "unsettling and undeniable" disregard for the truth and a new information environment in which "lies, as well as truths, now circulate at speeds we can't comprehend."[2] If the current moment has revived the prospect that power could still have the "last say" on the fate of factual truth, the best antidote to this threat remains our institutional capacity for independent investigation, largely carried out by a bold and scrupulous free press. For all we keep hearing about how the Brave New World of social media and its unknowns are a major threat to American democracy—the "disease vector," if you will—the real question may be whether the established U.S. media is up to the confluence of challenges that define the current moment.

"I'm Going to Suck All the Oxygen out of the Room"

It took Donald Trump less than a year and a half in office to pass the 3,200 mark in false or misleading statements as president—after a campaign in which he lied and dissembled almost incessantly.[3] Trump, as a candidate and as president, has served up a stream of lies, falsehoods, distortions, and misdirection at a superhuman rate; moreover, he has distinguished himself through the *repetition* of his lies and distortions. Not only has he been thoroughly unchastened when members of the media have produced facts and information contradicting his lies, but he has constantly leapt at the opportunity to continue lying in their faces. Indeed, it has long been a central facet of Trump's approach that he regularly goes on to repeat falsehoods dozens of times after they've been widely debunked by major news organizations. At his campaign rallies, Trump regularly taunted and abused reporters, sometimes singling them out personally, egging on crowds to join in the vitriol. This, too, arguably got worse once Trump was elected, given that such attacks on the media—when waged by the president himself—amount to a direct effort to weaken the role of an institution that is supposed to hold elected officials like him accountable.

The media's traditional gatekeeping role has been declining in recent years due to the rise of alternative sources like talk radio, the internet, blogs, and social media giants—and as a candidate, Trump exploited this erosion with remarkable skill and dedication, particularly through use of his Twitter feed. This bull and bluster has only continued now that Trump lives in the White House. Indeed, it has arguably intensified in the face of widespread concern—including among his own advisers—about the destructive potential of off-the-cuff tweets coming from the president of the United States.[4]

Trump's approach to the news media has long rested on a core insight: He can circumvent the media while at the same time exploiting its worst collective and institutional instincts to his own great benefit. In late 2013, well over a year before he declared his candidacy, Trump privately made a brash prediction to a roomful of politicians in his home state of New York. As one of his listeners recounted to *Politico*, Trump told the assembled that once he got in the race, "I'm going to suck all the oxygen out of the room. I know how to work the media in a way that they will never take the lights off of me."[5]

As this is secondhand testimony, we don't know for certain that Trump made that remark. But Trump's conduct in the years since leaves little doubt that the quote accurately conveys what has long been one of his animating sentiments, and his instinct in this regard turned out to be entirely correct. During the GOP primaries, Trump received a level of saturation coverage that undoubtedly helped him prevail over his rivals. One study found that disproportionately extensive coverage early on when his poll numbers were low subsequently helped him overcome that deficit and go on to win the nomination.[6] Indeed, Jeff Zucker, the president of CNN, subsequently admitted his network had erred in this regard. "If we made any mistake last year, it's that we probably did put on too many of his campaign rallies in those early months and let them run," he said in October 2016. Zucker even admitted that Trump's unpredictability had made it harder for them to resist: "Because you never knew what he would say, there was an attraction to put those on the air."[7] In other words, Trump played to the networks' worst instincts—exploiting their fascination with crude, ratings-driving spectacle to draw far more free media attention than was paid to his rivals. Worse, because so few journalists took his chances seriously, Trump used the networks to get his message out unfiltered, even as he largely escaped probing scrutiny until it was too late.

Unfortunately, once Trump became president, there were plenty of signs that the networks hadn't sufficiently learned from their mistake. Trump continued to hold rallies and, on repeated occasions, the networks aired them live, broadcasting his lies to the nation with no filter or fact checking. The networks carried one Trump rally in March 2018 live for over an hour, according to *Washington Post* media columnist Margaret Sullivan. "For Trump, free TV time is not only pure political gold, but also an opportunity to insult, to abuse, and to spread falsehoods," Sullivan noted acidly, adding that for the ratings-minded networks, the "profits-above-all line of thinking is alive and well."[8]

During the campaign, Trump told lies at a far greater rate than did his rival, Hillary Clinton. But also important and telling were the differences in how the two campaigns treated the *institutional role* of the media in our political system. During the summer of 2016, *Washington Post* fact checker Glenn Kessler noted that the Clinton campaign readily responded to fact-checking queries and regularly tried to provide documentation of her claims on the campaign trail. By contrast, Kessler reported, Trump's staff rarely responded to such queries and almost never even bothered trying to back up his claims.[9] This pattern was visible everywhere throughout the campaign. Yet the general tone suffusing much of the coverage was that both candidates were dishonest, creating an equivalence where there just wasn't one. Though this started to change toward the end of the race, news organizations—in a quest for superficial balance that ironically ended up portraying a deeply misleading picture—were generally reluctant to treat Trump's level of lying and contempt for the press's core function as something fundamentally different from Clinton's exercises in straying from the truth, which, despite the constant pillorying of her as calculating and cynical, had much more in common with the sort of conventional dishonesty routinely displayed by politicians. Trump exploited that reluctance brilliantly.

The Media as "the Enemy of the American People"

All of these things—Trump's success in going around traditional media gatekeepers; his ferocious attacks on the media; his continued exploitation of the networks' willingness to continue carrying his rallies live; and his nonstop lying—have created a widespread sense that in Trump, the news media are confronting something fundamentally new and different. Just after his victory, which shocked most media observers, this feeling became particularly pronounced, as Trump and his team immediately displayed in the early days of the administration their intention to keep up with these tactics. Trump set the tone early on, blasting the media for supposedly minimizing the size of the lackluster crowds at his inauguration. Soon after, in a tweet in February 2017, Trump labeled the media the "enemy of the American people." He has kept up the attacks ever since, describing the press as everything from "disgusting" to "lying" to "failing" to his most-often-applied epithet, "fake news." In 2018, Trump, seeking to punish *The Washington Post*, repeatedly attacked the corporate behemoth Amazon, temporarily driving down its stock price, because Amazon owner Jeff Bezos also owns the newspaper. Even some Trump administration officials privately conceded that his attacks came in response to *Post* articles that he didn't like,[10] meaning he openly employed the presidential bully pulpit to attack a private company to chill media efforts to hold him accountable. And it wasn't just print journalism that infuriated Trump: out of seeming animosity toward CNN, his administration tried to block the merger of Time Warner (CNN's parent company) and AT&T. The effort was unsuccessful, but through these moves, Trump sent a clear signal: Trump was willing to employ the power of his office to target media companies whose coverage displeased and angered him.

It's true that former presidents have attacked the press, perhaps most notably Richard Nixon, who privately vilified the media and had his vice president publicly deliver withering assaults on the major networks. But one careful examination of Trump's rhetoric toward the media—by RonNell Andersen Jones and Lisa Grow Sun, law professors at the University of Utah and Brigham Young University—concluded that Trump had broken new ground by attacking the press through a process of "enemy construction," which casts the press as a *fundamentally illegitimate* enemy of the people. For authoritarians in the strongman style such as Trump, "the people" is generally a fungible category understood, tacitly or overtly, as those groups who support the leader—you're either with him or against him. Since (in his eyes) the press is Trump's enemy, it is therefore the enemy of his followers—"the people"—as well. This is a break with Trump's predecessors, who fought with the media but essentially maintained grudging respect for its institutional role in our democracy. As Jones and Sun concluded, the Trump administration's crossing of this threshold "should be recognized for the dire risks that it poses" to the "special functions the press performs for the wider public" as an institution in our democracy.[11]

To a degree that defies comparison to other politicians, Trump relentlessly appears to wield his dishonesty as a species of power, as an overt way of exercising maximum dominance. Trump's lying isn't about winning an argument with his opponents or even casting doubt on their records in conventional political ways but rather about obliterating them through merciless personal belittlement. More broadly, Trump isn't trying to persuade anyone to believe his lies as much as he's trying to render factual reality irrelevant—thus reducing the pursuit of agreement on it to just another part of the media circus in which he thrives. He's asserting the power to roll over constraints normally imposed by expectations of fealty to basic norms, such as the notion that our political discourse should be shaped around a good-faith empirical effort to strive toward a common understanding of facts, and the idea that the press has an important institutional role in making that shared understanding possible.

There is a reason Trump regularly tells lies that are very easy to debunk: The whole point of them is to assert the power to say what the truth is, even when—or *especially* when—easily verifiable facts, ones that are right in front of our noses, dictate the contrary. The brazenness and shamelessness of his lying is not just a by-product of an effort to mislead voters that Trump is merely taking to new levels. Rather, the brazenness and shamelessness of the lying is central to his broader project of declaring for himself the power to say what reality is.

Tony Schwartz, who spent hundreds of hours around Trump when he ghostwrote Trump's 1987 self-hagiography, *The Art of the Deal*, has even declared that Trump's lying is often tantamount to a pathological effort at dominance. Observing Trump's presidency, Schwartz explained that when Trump's claims are challenged, he "instinctively doubles down," even when they are "demonstrably false," even in defending lies of the most trivial nature. ("His aim is never accuracy; it's domination," Schwartz added.)[12] Trump's instinct to lie was surely honed by his years as a television star. Academics who study reality TV have noted that Trump's treatment of the truth as a politician often draws on the techniques of the genre. Such shows give the appearance of being unfiltered and raw but are in fact highly staged and edited. The plotlines of *The Apprentice* showcased Trump as a brilliant and infallible character who forced everyone to react to him through the wielding of outsize and outrageous statements.[13] The show reinforced another ugly Trumpian instinct: that media built around celebrating Donald Trump was the real arbiter of truth. Indeed, Trump spent years sharpening his ability to declare what reality is not just as a reality TV personality but also as a real estate figure who worked over New York's tabloids—which together honed his talent for employing *entertaining and attention-grabbing* falsehoods, which he then weaponized in politics, albeit for uglier and more sinister ends.

Finally, Trump's relentless lying is also an extension of his authoritarian tendencies. As the McGill University political theorist Jacob Levy has observed, Trump's approach is best understood through the lens employed by "the great analysts of truth and speech under totalitarianism," such as Arendt and George Orwell, who have demonstrated that often "a leader with authoritarian tendencies will lie" with the express purpose of getting others to "repeat his lie."[14] The lies, Levy notes, are "demonstrations of power" that are expressly designed to "undermine the existence of shared belief in truth and facts."[15]

Here it's worth returning to Arendt. In a 1974 interview, she expounded on the power of lies to erode the relevance of reality itself, in a manner that more than four decades later applies perfectly to Trump's approach:

> If everybody always lies to you, the consequence is not that you believe the lies, but rather that nobody believes anything any longer. . . . a people that no longer can believe anything cannot make up its mind. It is

> deprived not only of its capacity to act but also of its capacity to think and to judge. And with such a people you can then do what you please.[16]

Thus, in Arendt's telling, it is a threat to democracy when "nobody believes anything any longer." There is little question that Trump—whether instinctually or consciously—sees such an outcome as precisely his goal.

Declining Confidence in the Media—Mostly a Republican Phenomenon?

The widely discussed decline in public confidence in "the media" is to some degree based on a flawed concept. After all, "the media" is in no sense a monolith. As Derek Thompson, a writer for *The Atlantic*, has put it, the media is more akin to an "information galaxy, a vast and complex star system composed of diverse and opposing organizations," which are themselves composed of "flawed media merchants, with individual strengths, weaknesses, biases, and blindspots."[17] And yet there *is* some sense in which "the media" does exist. The media, for our purposes (and for those who view it as the enemy), is composed mainly of the major national newspapers and broadcast and cable networks—that is, the constellation of reporters, editors, pundits, commentators, and talk-show hosts who, day in and day out, provide the material for, and give shape to, the national political conversation. By investing substantial resources in trying to hold public officials accountable through aggressive information gathering that hews to generally agreed upon professional standards, these entities in effect combine into a single institution, one that is "liberal," at least in the sense that its members are loosely but imperfectly devoted to an Enlightenment tradition of empiricism and objectivity, and view themselves as playing an important role in liberal democracy, by keeping voters informed about public matters and holding political actors accountable.

It is true that public confidence in the media as an institution is declining, a fact that Trump has both exploited and sought to deliberately exacerbate. The story of this decline has been told in many other places, so I'll only briefly recap the causes that have been ascribed to it. They include the press's tendency to cover politics like a sport with an insufficient focus on policy; the fracturing of the media in the information age, which has made it easier for people to seek out media outlets that tell them what they want to hear, leading them to distrust the very idea that major news organizations possess some kind of institutional authority; and the broader decline of public faith in our institutions. But it's important to appreciate the degree to which this reflects a trend *among Republicans*, as opposed to among overall Americans. The Pew Research Center—which has collected data going back decades that is widely seen as a good gauge of confidence in the media—developed a set of trend lines and charts that shed light on these public attitudes in various ways.

Since 1985, Pew has asked respondents whether they believe "news organizations' criticism of political leaders keeps them from doing things that shouldn't be done." This is Pew's way of determining whether respondents believe the news media is functioning as an effective watchdog—that is, imposing effective accountability—on public officials. A large majority of overall Americans—70 percent—continue to believe this as of 2017. The chart below shows these numbers shift among Republicans and Democrats, depending on which party has captured the White House. The last time there was a GOP president, this sentiment dropped substantially among Republicans. Under Trump, it has hit a *record low*:

2017 revealed the sharpest divide ever measured in support of the news media's watchdog role

% of U.S. adults who think that criticism from news organizations keeps political leaders from doing things that shouldn't be done

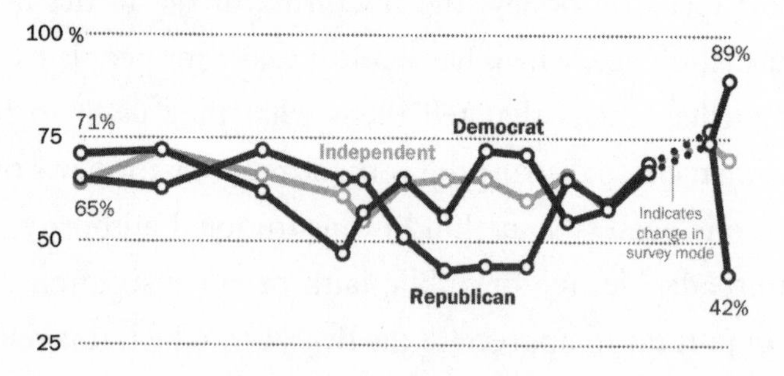

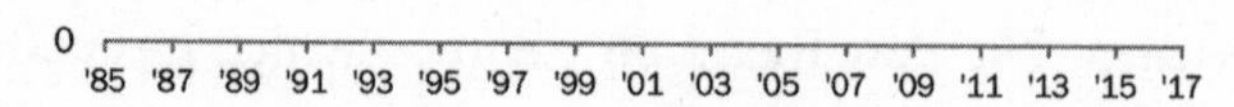

Note: Dotted line indicates a change in mode. Polls from 1985-2013 were conducted via phone. In 2016 and 2017, the polls were conducted on the American Trends Panel, which is online.
Source: Surveys conducted 1985-2017.
"Americans' Attitudes About the News Media Deeply Divided Along Partisan Lines"
PEW RESEARCH CENTER

Pew also finds that since 1985, Republicans have consistently said in larger percentages that the news media favors one side. Under Trump, this has hit a *record high:*

Republicans consistently more likely to say news media favor one side

% of U.S. adults who say that news organizations tend to favor one side when presenting the news on political and social issues

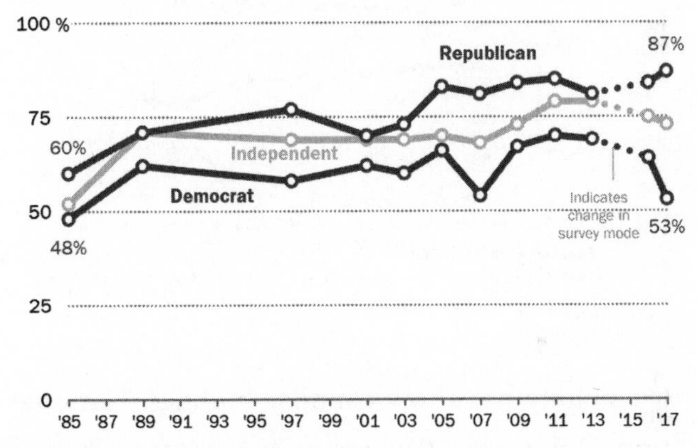

Note: Dotted line indicates a change in mode. Polls from 1985-2013 were conducted via phone. In 2016 and 2017, the polls were conducted on the American Trends Panel, which is online.
Source: Surveys conducted 1985-2017.
"Americans' Attitudes About the News Media Deeply Divided Along Partisan Lines"
PEW RESEARCH CENTER

Finally, going back to 2010, Republicans have consistently said in lower percentages that the news media have a "positive" effect on the way things are going in this country. These also hit low points in 2016 (during the presidential campaign) and 2017 (during Trump's first year in office):

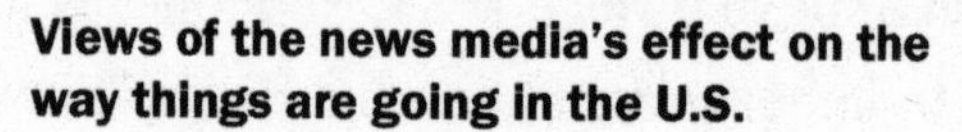

% who say the national news media have a positive effect on the way things are going in the country

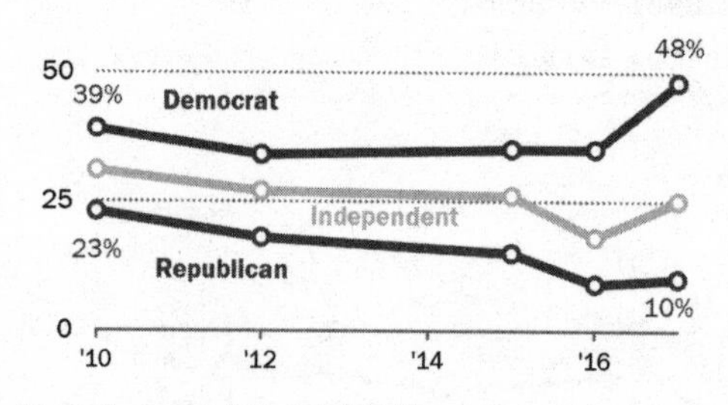

Source: Surveys conducted 2010-2017.
"Sharp Partisan Divisions in Views of National Institutions"
PEW RESEARCH CENTER

Other polling has shown similar findings. National surveys from Quinnipiac University, for instance, have regularly found that majorities of overall Americans trust the news media over Trump to tell them the truth about important issues. But Quinnipiac has also found that unsettlingly large majorities *of Republicans* view it the other way around: They trust Trump, rather than the news media, to tell them the truth.[18] This is a terrible development. It is precisely what Trump is *trying* to accomplish.

But here again, the story long predates Trump. Over the last few decades, a massive media infrastructure has arisen on the right—one that includes talk radio and blogs and websites and, at the center of it all, Fox News—that has both sought to counterprogram the major news organizations and destroy their credibility in the minds of Republican voters. As Brian Beutler, a writer for the progressive website Crooked Media, has observed, "a major project of the conservative movement over the last 30 years has been to convince Republican voters that mainstream media organizations" are "little more than private-sector satellite arms of the Democratic Party," with the result that these efforts have "successfully siloed" the "conservative masses."[19] This has essentially rendered these voters unreachable, in the sense that they simply no longer place any credibility in the very idea that the big news organizations are conducting good-faith information and news-gathering efforts. By some measures, the effort has largely worked: Pew polling has found that conservative voters are far more reliant on a single partisan media source—yup, you guessed it, Fox News—than are liberal voters, who tend to rely on more media sources, including major news organizations.[20] (Indeed, in one sense this rebounded on "Never Trump" Republicans and conservatives: It was so successful that they were unable to stop him in 2016 in part because mainstream news criticism had been discredited among GOP voters and thus aggressive reporting on Trump didn't have a sufficient impact among them.)

Still, the Trump era, this has reached new levels. We have seen the rise of what Axios media reporter Sara Fischer aptly termed the "pro-Trump media machine." This machine doesn't merely fluff Trump and attack his enemies; it also relentlessly amplifies Trump's assaults on the conventional press. For instance, in the spring of 2018 the news broke that local anchors at Sinclair Broadcast Group, the largest owner of local TV stations in America, were reading from the same script, one that accused "national media outlets" of broadcasting "fake stories," a claim that was widely criticized as a propagandistic amplification of Trump's own "fake news" refrain. As Fischer noted, "pro-Trump media" is "disseminating Trumpian rhetoric about fake news and mainstream media bias" through an ever-multiplying profusion of media channels. Not only this, but many pro-Trump media figures—most prominently Fox News' Sean Hannity, who reportedly speaks to Trump regularly—also constantly counterprogram the mainstream press's reporting about the ongoing investigation into Russian sabotage of our election and alleged Trump campaign collaboration with it, as well as the mainstream press's regular drumbeat of reporting about Trump's efforts to obstruct that investigation, with nonstop attacks on the credibility of the investigators and on the news outlets themselves. It all smacked of an elaborate, many-tentacled propaganda campaign designed to create an alternate reality of the Russia probe in the minds of millions of Trump supporters—one in which shadowy "Deep State" intelligence operatives and the mainstream media are conspiring to stage a coup to remove Trump from power—in apparent preparation for political battle over that investigation's final revelations, and, possibly, over whether Trump will ever be held accountable for them. During the battles of the Watergate era, Nixon didn't have anything comparable at his disposal. Whatever happens with the Russia investigation, the long-term implications for our democracy of such a massive domestic disinformation campaign designed to delegitimize major U.S. institutions in the minds of millions of Americans remain uncertain.

All this is driven in no small part by Trump himself. But he has all kinds of help, due to changing information technology.

The Anxiety of the Disinformation Scientists

One thing that is remarkable about the massive amount of misinformation and disinformation coursing through our politics is how little we know about it. (*Misinformation* is unintentionally false or inaccurate information, while *disinformation* is intentionally false information deliberately crafted and spread to mislead.) As it happens, this conundrum has attracted the attention of numerous scholars from a range of disciplines, who tend to focus on the technological side of the problem, such as the sudden advent of Facebook, Twitter, and other social media, explosions of "fake news" and relentless impostor "bots" (short for *robots*, which some academics describe as "automated accounts that post based on algorithms"), and the increasing ease of video and audio manipulation. Compounding the confusion, all of these online pathologies have come alongside other big developments, such as the successful sabotage of the 2016 election by Russians via an elaborate campaign of information warfare. As part of a Department of Justice investigation, thirteen Russian nationals were indicted in early 2018 for a scheme to sabotage the election in Trump's favor that included the extensive use of Facebook to post ads and content designed to stoke political division and confusion among U.S. voters[21]—a disconcerting example of how these various misinformation and disinformation trends and developments overlap with one another.

Faced with this siege of misinformation and disinformation, various types of researchers are struggling to make empirical sense of what is happening. There are computer scientists who are trying to figure out how—and through what sort of networks—misinformation and disinformation spread on the internet. There are psychologists and cognitive scientists studying how people are processing all the misinformation and disinformation and whether corrections are effective in dissuading people of false beliefs. There are political scientists who are grappling with how these phenomena are impacting political polarization and deliberation. In multiple fields, academics are holding conferences, debating on LISTSERVs, and churning out papers. To eavesdrop on these conversations and read through these papers is to be humbled by the vast challenges posed by the current moment—specifically, how much more we have to do to understand what it all means.

Take, for instance, "fake news," which has been described by one group of academics as "fabricated information that mimics news media content." Fake news comes from many sources, including hostile foreign actors and freelance operators in the United States who are either politically motivated or are just trying to spread confusion for sport, and have varying degrees of clout. It has been well established that social media enabled the viral spread of fake news during the 2016 election. One widely cited study, by BuzzFeed News, found that in the final three months of the campaign, the twenty top-performing fake news stories generated more shares and engagement on Facebook than did the twenty top-performing real news stories from major journalistic outlets. All but three of the top fake news stories were pro-Trump and anti-Clinton.[22] To play on the old Stephen Colbert saw that "reality has a well-known liberal bias," fake news has a pro-Trump bias.

But gauging the actual *impact* of fake news on information consumers—and by extension, on our democracy—remains an elusive task. A team of political scientists from Princeton, Dartmouth, and the University of Exeter analyzed the internet histories of thousands of users in the lead-up to the 2016 election. They found that approximately one in four Americans was exposed to fake news—a disconcertingly huge number of people. But such stories constituted only a very tiny fraction of those people's overall media consumption, which was overwhelmingly dominated by real news. What's more, a large percentage of the aggregate consumption of fake news was heavily concentrated among less than one tenth of Americans. (Since not all Americans are voters, the pool of impacted voters might be even smaller.) That's good news. But even here, the researchers conceded that their findings were dramatically limited. They also acknowledged that a great deal of work needs to be done to understand *what impact* exposure to fake news actually has on its consumers in the first place.[23]

The same goes for bots. It is now widely established that they are prevalent in disinformation campaigns all around the world. One study found that in the run-up to the 2016 election, around 400,000 bots on Twitter were involved in the political chatter about the election, producing around 3.8 million tweets—or *one fifth of the entire Twitter conversation.*[24] During the 2016 campaign, bots disguised as personal accounts of what turned out to be imaginary individuals were heavily involved in spreading fake news, since actual humans regularly retweeted fake news stories posted by con artist software, meaning humans are, in a way, subject to manipulation through the use of bots.[25] (One of the humans who retweets bot-posted fake news is the current president of the United States.) Some of this bot activity formed part of the disinformation operation run by Russians to assist Trump and hurt Hillary Clinton, and other Russian bot activity has sought to amplify social divisions since the election—for instance, after white supremacist protests turned violent in Charlottesville, Virginia.[26] Bot activity, of course, is not even remotely confined to operations run by Russia or even other national states; entire shadow industries in bot activity for purely commercial purposes have developed, and countless individuals have launched their own bot armies for all sorts of purposes, as the software for doing so is extremely easy to procure. By one estimate, bots run tens of millions of Twitter accounts.[27] These sorts of statistics—especially the fact that it is often impossible to know if you are interacting with a real person or a piece of software that has been designed to fool you—are a big reason why Twitter and Facebook (which has admitted to tens of millions of fake accounts, too[28]) have faced withering criticism since the election for failing to police such malicious activity.

Scary, for sure. But how much do bots really matter to our democracy? We just don't know. One study in early 2018 analyzed the spread online of over 100,000 news stories—true and false—that had been tweeted millions of times. It concluded that the fake news stories had spread faster than the real ones did. But bots were responsible for spreading both the true and false stories at similar rates, while human beings are the ones who spread the fake news faster, which the study's authors surmised was partly driven by its novelty value. To paraphrase a quote often erroneously attributed to Mark Twain, in the new information ecosystem, it is truer than ever that a lie can travel around the world faster than the truth can put on its shoes—but bots may be less to blame for this than we human beings are. "Although more and more of our access to information and news is guided by these new technologies, we know little about their contribution to the spread of falsity online," the study's authors concluded."[29]

Worries about the online encouragement and spread of bogus claims and fictitious information crystallized in an attention-getting manifesto signed in early 2018 by a multidisciplinary team of scientists, arguing that the rise of fake news has become a "global" problem that reflects an "erosion of long-standing institutional bulwarks against misinformation in the internet age." Lamenting that "much remains unknown regarding the vulnerabilities of individuals, institutions, and society to manipulations by malicious actors," they called for a broad collaboration between researchers and social media giants like Facebook and Google to "redesign our information ecosystem in the 21st century."[30]

I contacted the lead author of that manifesto, David Lazer, a professor of political, computer, and information science at Northeastern University, who is widely considered a cutting-edge researcher on these matters, and asked him to spell out just how much we *do not* know. His answer to me is worth reproducing at length:

> We have a long way to go. We don't have a firm handle on *how much* misinformation there is. We can't even answer the question, is there more than there was 20 years ago? We don't know whether the misinformation out there is changing attitudes or behaviors. We do know that we're more polarized. But we don't exactly know *why* that is. We don't know what is caus-

> ing political polarization. A big question is whether social media is playing a role in that. We don't know whether misinformation is enabling that polarization, or whether it's merely a symptom of it. I certainly wouldn't say that we know nothing. But we don't know much.

Lazer concluded that this whole new world of online misinformation and disinformation is "mostly a universe of dark matter."[31] Okay, but given that the light of truth is worth pursuing, what do we do now?

Can Journalism Adapt?

One salutary recent development has been that some news organizations have embarked on an increasingly aggressive up-front effort to signal to readers when politicians—particularly Trump—try to mislead or lie to them. Cable news networks have more regularly taken to labeling statements as "false" right in their chyrons (the caption superimposed over the lower part of a video image) as they air footage of politicians making those statements, so viewers almost instantly learn they're being deceived. (It's worth noting that social media tends to amplify this effect: Ordinary viewers and other journalists sometimes tweet out visual screen captures of such chyrons, further informing those who might encounter the lie in question at a later point.) And multiple big news organizations have begun to label politicians' statements as false right in their headlines far more often than in the past. For example, during the controversy over the Trump administration's policy of separating immigrant children from their families at the border, the president repeatedly lied about who was to blame. One of the *New York Times*' lead stories on this was headlined "Trump Repeats Falsehood That Democrats Are to Blame for Separating Migrant Families."[32] There have been many such examples.

It's notable that such labeling comes more naturally to news outlets that came of age in the internet era. BuzzFeed News, for instance, has adopted a policy of calling out falsehoods in headlines, which by itself is not original, but what's particularly interesting about its approach is that it is grounded in an appreciation of the specific perils of the current moment. "The importance of headlines is arguably even greater now in the social media era, because a lot of people are in passive consumption mode," Craig Silverman, the media editor at BuzzFeed News, told me. "When people see stuff on social media, what they often see is only the headlines. If you are restating claims that are false or misleading in headlines, you are spreading misinformation. And social media is pouring gasoline on that fire."[33]

This is a crucial insight, and while things have gotten better in recent months, it remains one that plenty of traditional journalists and news organizations still refuse to take seriously enough. You constantly see headlines on news organizations' websites that blare forth a politician's false, dubious, or unsupported claims without informing readers that those claims are, well, false or dubious or unsupported. Often it requires reading deep into a story to discover it when there is even any corrective at all. The same goes for news organizations' Twitter feeds—tweets alerting readers to breaking news regularly transmit false claims with no correctives in the tweets themselves. It is a great irony of this moment that, by broadcasting forth Trump's lies—while declining to inform readers that they are just that, or by burying the truth deep within its accompanying articles—the news organizations that Trump regularly derides actually are spreading a species of fake news—that is, fake news authored by Trump himself. There is little doubt that a deceiver as prolific and innovative as Trump grasps—whether instinctively or consciously—that those getting news from social media and on mobile devices often read no further than headlines or tweets, and that transmitting out disinformation that gets amplified in headlines and news feeds help him exploit this facet of the shifting information landscape.

Yet despite these obvious dangers, too many newspaper editors and television producers still continue to fear that if they forcefully—and prominently—call out Trump's lies for what they are, they will somehow come across as biased or lacking in objectivity. Indeed, some editors have offered the tortured argument that they should refrain from using the word *lie* because it suggests knowledge of Trump's *in-*

tent to mislead, which cannot be conclusively established.[34] But this rigs the game in Trump's favor: One cannot ever conclusively *prove* whether Trump is intentionally lying, as opposed to just delusional or hopelessly uninformed. Yet if Trump repeats a falsehood over and over after it has been debunked, it is obviously deliberate deception; if news organizations refrain from calling this out as such, they are failing to accurately describe what is right there in plain sight. This misleads readers and viewers not just in each particular case. Importantly, it also misleads them more broadly about the truly sinister and deliberate nature of Trump's ongoing and concerted campaign to obliterate the possibility of shared agreement on facts and on the news media's legitimate institutional role in keeping voters informed. The resulting standard for describing Trump does not reckon seriously with the scale of the challenge to the truth he poses, and, by portraying his ongoing campaign of flood-the-zone lying as conventional dishonesty or mere incompetence, paints a profoundly misleading picture of the realities of the current moment.

Some journalists have actually begun to publicly acknowledge this. In a remarkable on-air moment in the spring of 2018, NBC's Andrea Mitchell conceded that older traditions of journalism might not be up to that challenge. "It's very uncomfortable for a lot of people of my generation of journalists to constantly be saying, 'the president misrepresented,' 'he misspoke,' 'this is a lie,' 'this is not true,'" Mitchell said. "But people have to speak out." This is great to see, but wasn't this obvious to Mitchell's colleagues a year ago? Heck, what about two years ago?

What's more, some journalists have taken their institutional responsibility to avoid abetting the spreading of disinformation very seriously for some time now. CNN's Jake Tapper, for instance, has regularly called out falsehoods—and "lies"—on all sides, but he has flatly declared that the most pressing attacks on the truth right now are "far more prevalent on the right" and come most prominently from "the president of the United States and his enablers and supporters."[35]

Meanwhile, plenty of journalists have come up with various other innovative responses to our current challenges. Faced with the relentless crush of Trump's dishonesty, numerous news organizations have created interactive tools, such as databases, that enable readers to keep track of all his lies and distortions. *The Washington Post* fact-checking team's database, for instance, sorts all of Trump's lies and distortions by chronology, and even by the number of times he repeats the falsehood in question. Other outlets have broken ground in other creative ways. The independent investigative nonprofit ProPublica, for instance, has worked hard to develop new models of journalism that include collaborating with other news outlets (rather than merely viewing them as competitors) to pool investigative resources in an effort to keep track of the Trump administration's many corruption scandals, and an unusually aggressive effort by its reporters to both exhibit transparency about the reporting process to readers and enlist their help in information gathering. ProPublica has also excelled at detailed reporting on how Trump's policies—such as his nightmarish deportations—have directly impacted real people, and notably has organized all this reporting in a very user-friendly way on the web. Such a focus on real-world consequences can help break the political conversation out of the din of Twitter-fueled disinformation.

Another model to counter that roar of disinformation has been developed to great effect by David Fahrenthold, the bespectacled, unassuming *Washington Post* reporter who stumbled onto a new approach to journalism in the Trump era that would ultimately win him a Pulitzer Prize. In early 2016, Trump, then just another GOP presidential primary candidate, began giving away oversize prop checks in the name of his charity, for which he had raised millions of dollars. Fahrenthold started following the money and soon learned that Trump had stopped handing over the money well before distributing all he had raised.[36] Fahrenthold then dug deeper into Trump's past pattern of charitable giving, calling on Twitter followers to join in the sleuthing. He posted photographs of pen-scrawled pages from his reporter's notebook on Twitter to demonstrate for readers how his reporting was going. He ultimately documented a broad pattern going back years in which many of Trump's claims of philanthropy had been exaggerated or made up. Adapting a form of crowdsource reporting previously pioneered by blogs, Fahrenthold developed a new template for the use of social media for unearthing the truth. This hints at a way that working journalists, by showing transparency and using social media to interact with readers, can try to shore up public confidence in the press at a moment when it's under assault. And it suggests constructive ways for ordinary readers to join with journalists in the battle against the lies and disinformation that threaten to swamp our democracy.

We've Been Here Before

Early in the Trump presidency, Jay Rosen, the liberal media critic and New York University journalism professor, wrote a series of prescient essays arguing that Trump and his allies were already carrying out—and would continue carrying out—a concerted and deliberate assault on the media's *core institutional role* in our democracy. In response, Rosen argued, media figures needed to rise to this challenge by committing themselves to a new "public mindset," one that forthrightly confronts the need to mount a concerted public defense of the news media's core liberal democratic values. "Like it or not, the press is a public actor, currently in the fight of its life," Rosen wrote. "Nothing in their training or temperament prepares journalists to fight the kind of battle they're in." As a result, journalists needed to focus on bigger questions about the institutional function of their profession with the ultimate goal of getting more people to reappreciate journalism's role as an indispensable and "independent" actor in our democracy.[37]

There have been plenty of signs that leading journalists grasp the need to redouble their commitment to these fundamental values. CNN media reporter Brian Stelter reported in the spring of 2018 that within the country's newsrooms, there is "more and more introspection" about the media's response to the deception tactics employed by Trump and his allies, and about the question of whether the press is compounding the "damage" by airing and repeating falsehoods without any adequate institutional response to it.[38] Several leading figures in journalism have given speeches emphasizing the need to respond to the moment by rethinking their profession's core commitments.[39] It should also be stressed that in many ways, news organizations have let the quality of their journalism do the talking, and in this respect, the press has performed magnificently, breaking all kinds of stories about Trump's corruption and double-dealing and his behind-the-scenes efforts to derail the Department of Justice investigation into his campaign's collusion with Russia. But ordinary Americans and news consumers have a role to play here as well. They can be aware of the deeper precariousness of this moment for journalism's core institutional role, and they can use social media to push back on attacks designed to undermine that role, as well as lend public support to quality journalism and journalists who are speaking out publicly in ways designed to fortify their profession's institutional function.

American journalism has confronted other such moments before. In the late 1960s and early 1970s, the profession was tested in then-new ways by a confluence of cultural and political changes, including the growth of the federal government and mass media; the increasing transparency of Congress via innovations such as the Freedom of Information Act; and the massive official deception around the Watergate scandal and the Vietnam War. As the previously mentioned media scholar Michael Schudson recounts, journalists and the news media adapted by becoming more probing and analytical and by asserting themselves more aggressively toward powerful figures, changes that brought a "new skepticism and critical instinct to journalism," which enabled the profession of journalism to evolve along with changes in American society and political culture.[40]

We may be in the midst of another such transition. As outlined above, the news media seems to be retaining its institutional independence and appears to be finding new ways to meet the brutal new challenges it faces. But as Arendt put it back when Trump was only twenty-one years old, truth and politics are perpetually "on rather bad terms with each other. Factual truth is fragile in politics, and its survival is never guaranteed." As we are learning all over again, it always remains possible that "power will have the last say."

6

Is Fair Play Possible in Our Politics?

During the 2016 presidential campaign, Donald Trump repeatedly called Hillary Clinton a criminal, and his chief allies frequently led rousing chants at rallies calling for her to be thrown in prison. In the lead-up to election day, Trump also repeatedly declared that if he lost, it could only reflect the outcome of a rigged election. What's made all of this even more unusual, however, is that Trump and his allies have kept up with these arguments *in victory*. As president, Trump has continued to insist that the vote tally amassed by Clinton was tainted by millions of illegally cast ballots—and that he actually won the popular vote—casting doubt on the legitimacy of her support.

In so doing, Trump has shredded a set of customs that play an important role in our democracy. After even the most bitterly contested elections, the winner and loser alike have tended to give gracious speeches acknowledging the validity of the outcome, followed by unifying gestures of various kinds on both sides. There is a reason for this. A hallmark of American stability has been the relatively peaceful transfer of power, which rests on expressions of respect for the legitimacy and political preferences of the opposition. Yet not only did Trump telegraph that he would cast any outcome in which he did not prevail as invalid; after winning, he continued to demonize the leader of the opposition as a criminal whose popular support was itself suspect. He has continued to call for the law enforcement apparatus he oversees as head of the executive branch to investigate Clinton on entirely fabricated grounds, transforming what may have just been dangerous campaign trail bluster into a very serious abuse of power.

Of course, in the real world, the political goodwill displayed by the customs that Trump shredded is to no small degree artificial, and in any case, it rarely lasts long. But the point is that we generally honor this ritual for a good reason: We want the losers and winners alike to feel as if the political competition in which they are participating is capable of producing outcomes that are legitimate, even if millions of people will inevitably be deeply disappointed or enraged or even horrified by the outcome. This ideally keeps some measure of social peace once political contestation resumes in the legislative arena. And—ideally—it bolsters faith in the system, enabling disappointed voters to look ahead to future elections with confidence that their ideas and aspirations will have a legitimate chance of prevailing.

Central to this confidence, to the degree that it exists, is the idea that our political competition, both in the electoral and legislative arenas, adheres to some baseline standard of *fair play*, as opposed to merely devolving into a naked power struggle in which anything goes. So let's not mince words about this: When President Trump continues to call for the power of law enforcement to be turned loose on his chief political opponent, and continues to claim that her popular support was suspect, he is declaring that politics *is* in fact a naked power struggle in which no outcomes are neutrally legitimate. This basic posture, of course, has driven—and has justified in the minds of his supporters—whatever tactics he deems necessary on his side, such as his relentless efforts to damage institutions designed to hold him accountable. It isn't just that for Trump, it's all a zero-sum war for dominance; it's also that there is no such thing as fair or neutral process.

This is, of course, what Trump has always been about. His business empire was built on skirting rules and laws, on scamming people who were vulnerable or lacked resources to legally defend themselves, and on operating with impunity wherever possible.[1] But now that Trump has transitioned from the business world to the presidency, this is no longer just about Trump's personal venality, corruption, and contempt for laws, rules, and constraints on his own conduct. In the political world, Trump both constitutes and is exacerbating a supercharging of all kinds of ongoing political degradations. Trump's assaults on the media are uniquely ferocious, but he undertook them in the full knowledge that Republican voters had been primed to hear them by decades of attacks on the media as corrupt and traitorous by Republican and conservative politicians and opinion makers. Trump revs up his voters with unprecedentedly (at least in recent times) naked displays of racism, nativism, ethnonationalism, and misogyny, but previous politicians used all manner of similar appeals—he simply employed a Trumpian bullhorn where a dog whistle had previously sufficed. Trump's treatment of the political opposition as corrupt and illegitimate is ferociously explicit, but in recent years there has been a dramatic escalation in mostly Republican efforts to rig elections via voter suppression and gerrymandering, as part of a broader deterioration in rules and norms governing the conduct of political competition that draws on the idea that because the opposition's legitimacy is dubious,[2] anything goes. Indeed, the very fact that so many Republican politicians have mutely fallen in line behind Trump as he stomps forward in all these ways confirms the point: They are perfectly comfortable embracing a type of raw and unbridled countermajoritarian power politics that now may be taking on a particularly ugly and authoritarian Trumpian gloss, but actually has been the festering ethos driving many Republican politicians for many years.

That raises two questions: Isn't the very idea that fair play is possible in politics hopelessly naive, given everything we've seen? If so, shouldn't Democrats and progressives accept this reality and adjust their goals and tactics accordingly?

Asymmetric Constitutional Hardball

The term *constitutional hardball* was originally coined by Mark Tushnet, a leading legal scholar at Harvard. He defined it as comprising political acts that are "within the bounds of existing constitutional doctrine" but are nonetheless seen as high-stakes behavior, because they represent an effort to fundamentally alter institutional relations to one party's advantage in some sense that violates previous understandings of the bounds of acceptable political combat.[3] Tushnet's theory (which is more complex than we need to get into here) has been heavily debated by academics for years. But outside the academy, journalists and politicos more generally use his term to denote tactics that are technically legal but are obviously questionable, flagrantly unscrupulous, or damaging to democratic relations.

There have been previous periods of constitutional hardball throughout U.S. history, of course. Among the examples Tushnet cites: In the late 1790s and early 1800s, the Federalists and the Democratic-Republicans waged scorched-earth warfare against each other, including trying to reshape the federal courts in their respective parties' favor. In the 1830s, Henry Clay, a foe of President Andrew Jackson, pushed the rechartering of the Bank of the United States years before it was necessary in order to create an issue against Jackson in the 1832 presidential election. (Jackson vetoed the rechartering and easily won reelection anyway.) In the 1930s, President Franklin Delano Roosevelt notoriously tried to pack the Supreme Court to overcome its opposition to his New Deal policies.

Most accounts locate the genesis of our current political unraveling with Newt Gingrich's ascension to the House speakership after the Republican Party's rout of Democrats in the 1994 midterm elections. Gingrich had spent years instructing his fellow Republicans to cast Congress as a deeply corrupt institution and to regularly attack Democrats as traitorous and anti-family, and it ultimately paid off. As speaker, Gingrich played constitutional hardball when he forced two government shutdowns. That ultimately backfired, bringing a period of relative bipartisan cooperation with President Bill Clinton, but while such cooperation got attention, behind the scenes Gingrich moved aggressively to undermine House committees whose staff had deep experience and long institutional memories, foreshadowing more recent GOP attacks on the neutral Congressional Budget Office. As political scientists Norm Ornstein and Thomas Mann recount in *It's Even Worse Than It Looks*, their seminal book on the evolution of the contemporary Republican Party, Gingrich's scorched-earth approach ended up having "a lasting impact on American politics." As they explain, it was Gingrich who put the GOP on a road to becoming "an insurgent outlier in American politics," one that is "ideologically extreme" and "scornful of compromise" and "dismissive of the legitimacy of its political opposition."[4]

In the late 1990s, the GOP's constitutional hardball culminated with the impeachment of Bill Clinton on charges of perjury and obstruction of justice stemming from a sexual harassment lawsuit against him. The hardball continued in 2001, when Senate Republicans axed their own chosen Senate parliamentarian—a kind of procedural referee—because his rulings angered them. And it continued in Texas and Colorado, when Republicans redrew their electoral maps in the middle of that decade to entrench their own power, a rarely employed form of political chicanery that foreshadowed a period of aggressively ramped-up gerrymandering after 2010 (chronicled in the next chapter). During the Obama presidency, Republican leaders escalated the hardball, forcing government shutdowns in a vain effort to roll back Obama's health care law, and pushing the level of filibustering to unprecedented levels. (Under Senate rules at the time, a minority could block legislation and nominations with a filibuster that could only be overcome by 60 Senate votes, creating a supermajority requirement to move bills or appointments forward.) Republicans flirted with financial calamity by threatening to refuse to raise the debt ceiling to try to force deep spending cuts. Per Tushnet's definition, none of what the Republicans were doing was technically illegal—but it pushed the procedural tactics far beyond the pale to hobble the Democrats, fair play be damned.

Senate majority leader Mitch McConnell also ruthlessly pushed GOP senators to maintain a blockade of united obstructionism to Obama's policies—even when those policies matched previous Republican initiatives. McConnell openly acknowledged that this strategy was expressly designed to deny Obama any bipartisan victories. "We worked very hard to keep our fingerprints off these proposals," he boasted to journalist Joshua Green, because "when you hang the 'bipartisan' tag on something, the perception is that differences have been worked out."[5] In other words, if any Republicans supported Obama's policies, the public would perceive them as having bipartisan legitimacy, which was to be denied at all costs. Most notorious was the Senate GOP's refusal to give any hearing at all to Obama's 2016 nominee to the Supreme Court—a nakedly cynical effort by McConnell to energize conservative voters in the 2016 election. When Trump won, this effort hit the judicial jackpot in conservative Supreme Court justice Neil Gorsuch.

After Trump's election, with Republicans in total control of the White House and Congress, the constitutional hardball has only continued or even gotten worse. House Republicans crafted a bill to repeal the Affordable Care Act—one that would result in tens of millions more people uninsured and revamp one sixth of the U.S. economy—under conditions of extraordinary secrecy, in spite of (or perhaps because of) the national outcry it unleashed. As part of their efforts, Republicans launched a full-scale assault on the neutral Congressional Budget Office—which strives for careful, detailed neutral analysis, in order to give lawmakers reliable information on which to base consequential decisions—because they found the CBO's findings politically inconvenient. They even passed a subsequent version of the bill before the CBO had a chance to weigh in on it.[6]

Again: this was not an attack on the Democrats, but a GOP assault on an agency known for dispassionate, nonpartisan fact-finding—revealing a long-running tendency among Republicans that predated Trump to toss aside neutral analysis when it doesn't suit Republican purposes.

Under Trump, the hardball has arguably metastasized into new forms, with congressional Republicans refining what might be described as *constitutional hardball by abdication*. When Trump took office, he refused to release his tax returns or to divest in his business holdings and immediately embarked on an extraordinary level of double-dealing and profiteering off the presidency—yet Republicans all but abandoned their oversight role on Trump's conduct and on multiple cabinet members who got ensnared in corruption scandals. (The very appointment of those cabinet members itself reflected a form of scorched-earth politics, as some of them were openly hostile to the core missions of the agencies they'd been tapped to run.) Republicans looked the other way as Trump compounded the kleptocracy with an extraordinary display of nepotism, installing his daughter Ivanka and son-in-law Jared Kushner in senior White House positions. Republicans actively blocked efforts by Democrats to try to force transparency around Trump's tax returns[7]—even though he and his family may have reaped enormous profits off the Republicans' tax overhaul of 2017,[8] and even though his returns might provide some insight into how Trump had been financially profiting from his presidency. And Trump's House GOP allies converted a congressional inquiry into possible Trump campaign collusion with Russia into a shadow effort to harass the investigation being run by the special counsel appointed by the Department of Justice, with the goal of providing Trump with a largely invented narrative of corruption in law enforcement that could provide a pretext for him to try to shut down that probe. Republicans perverted the congressional oversight process into a weapon on Trump's behalf, one devoted to delegitimizing—and thus shielding Trump from—efforts to hold him accountable.

To be sure, Democrats have played plenty of constitutional hardball of their own in the last few decades. Conservatives remain angry to this day about the hard-edged tactics Senate Democrats used to sink President Ronald Reagan's 1987 nomination of Robert Bork to the Supreme Court. Senate Democrats also undertook their own very real escalation of filibustering against President George W. Bush. Democrats pushed through the Affordable Care Act with procedural tactics that allowed it to pass the Senate with a simple majority (though that came after a genuine but failed effort to compromise with moderate Republican Senators). Following relentless GOP filibustering of Obama's nominees, Senate Democratic leaders did away with the filibuster on executive and judicial nominations other than to the Supreme Court (leaving the filibuster in place as a means for blocking legislation). Obama played plenty of constitutional hardball as well. He exercised executive authority to implement the health law in a manner that even some of its supporters have decried as possibly illegal.[9] Frustrated with the GOP Congress's inaction on immigration reform, he also undertook executive action that at a minimum pushed the procedural envelope in a big way to defer the deportation of millions of undocumented immigrants.[10]

So both sides have played plenty of constitutional hardball. But overall, Democratic efforts simply haven't been remotely equivalent to what we've seen from Republicans. It's true that such comparisons are hard to make in any kind of scientifically precise way. It's also true that over the years both sides routinely felt unfairly treated by the other. (Indeed, it is a key feature of these sorts of tactics that they often take on a tit-for-tat, reciprocal quality, which makes it very hard to assign overall blame for the ongoing deterioration.) But there's just no denying that while the constitutional hardball of the last few decades has been reciprocal, it has also been deeply unbalanced. In an important essay, law professors Joseph Fishkin and David Pozen undertook an exhaustive examination of both parties' conduct from the mid-1990s up through the present, and concluded that it has been marked by what they called "asymmetric constitutional hardball." After reviewing many of the episodes recounted above, they concluded that "Republican officials have been more willing than Democratic officials to play constitutional hardball . . . across a range of spheres," adding that "Democrats have also availed themselves of hardball throughout this period, but not with the same frequency or intensity." Fishkin and Pozen noted a fundamental asymmetry in the fact that some tactics had been employed by both sides (such as expansions of executive power and filibustering and other hard-edged legislative maneuvers), while others had been employed only by Republicans:

> Democrats have not threatened credibly to default on the national debt. They have not enacted measures likely to suppress Republican voter turnout in federal elections. They have not fired their own handpicked Senate Parliamentarian in an effort to overturn rulings that displeased them. They have not appointed agency heads that are known to oppose the agencies they will be leading. And they have not impeached a president. This tactical divide suggests there is a qualitative, not just a quantitative, difference in how the parties have been playing constitutional hardball—which we contend . . . is grounded in part in Republicans' greater willingness to incapacitate the government.[11]

Why the Two Parties Are Different

As noted in earlier chapters, a wide variety of metrics show that the two parties are more polarized than at perhaps any time since the Gilded Age. But the ideological pull on the two parties has not been equivalent. As political scientists Matt Grossmann and David Hopkins have demonstrated, one big part of this story centers on the different institutional structures that have built up on either side—structures that mean Republican lawmakers often find themselves under more pressure than Democratic lawmakers to engage in constitutional hardball and to adopt more uncompromising positions and tactics. Some of the more influential conservative groups, such as Americans for Prosperity, and the wealthy donors fueling them are generally unified around a common agenda—tax cuts, deregulation, shrinking government. By contrast, the larger liberal groups are distributed among an array of different issues, such as preserving the environment and improving access to women's health. On one side is a movement; on the other is a collection of interest groups. It is true that there are plenty of single-issue groups on the right (such as the National Rifle Association); and that there are groups on the left that try to pull Democrats to the left on many fronts (such as MoveOn and Indivisible). But as a general rule, ideologically conservative groups have a longer history than liberal groups do of viewing conventional bipartisan deal-making as a form of "selling out," and have been prone for far longer to demand scorched-earth tactics. Those groups, and the conservative grassroots, have had more success in organizing primary challenges to sitting GOP lawmakers than liberal groups and the grassroots have had when trying to displace elected Democrats, with the result that GOP lawmakers are driven far more by fear of primary challenges than Democratic lawmakers are. (There are some signs that a Trump-era progressive insurgency is starting to make life more uncomfortable for Democratic incumbents, such as when Alexandria Ocasio-Cortez shocked the political establishment by ousting a longtime House Democratic powerbroker from his New York district in the spring of 2018.)[12]

Driving much of this is the role and nature of the conservative media and the differences between Republicans' and Democrats' relationship with the mainstream news organizations. As we discussed in chapter 5, the media is more polarized and fragmented than ever, especially with the rise of the internet and social media. Both sides increasingly dwell in news and information bubbles, but this, too, shows signs of asymmetry. As we noted, Pew polling has shown that conservatives are far more dependent on a single news source—Fox News—than are liberals, who rely on a range of mainstream news outlets. (As we also noted, rising distrust in the news media may be a largely Republican phenomenon, reflecting decades of attacks on the media's validity from high-profile conservatives.) In their essay on asymmetric constitutional hardball, Fishkin and Pozen argue that conservative media are "more likely to explicitly or implicitly promote constitutional hardball" and to urge GOP lawmakers to "upend governmental norms" where necessary.[13] The narrative that GOP elites are betraying conservatism by not fighting hard enough for it has been a frequent staple of right-wing media, and GOP lawmakers live in constant fear of being labeled squishes or traitors to the cause.

Interestingly, this dynamic has become a source of *frustration* to progressives who want the Democratic Party to fight harder against Trump and Republicans now that Democrats are in the minority. Ben Wikler, the Washington director of MoveOn, told me a story that illustrates the point well. In early 2018, Democrats withheld their votes for a must-pass government funding bill in hopes of pressuring Republicans to agree to a measure legalizing hundreds of thousands of young undocumented immigrants brought here illegally as children. After the funding deadline passed, the government shut down, and a brutal spin war erupted over which party was to blame. Progressive groups like MoveOn were pressuring Democratic lawmakers to hold firm, presenting them with private polling showing that Trump and Republicans would ultimately take the blame for the shuttered government heading into a midterm election year, and thus would be forced to acquiesce. But Democrats caved within two days. The message that came back to progressive groups from Democratic lawmakers was that they were frightened of negative mainstream press coverage—a factor that just doesn't weigh as heavily on GOP lawmakers. "Moderate Democrats had their antennae tuned to the mainstream news environment, and how the shutdown was being framed by mass audience reporters," Wikler told me. "For Democrats, the idea of being labeled as irresponsible or obstructionist by a mainstream publication was a prospect too unbearable to contemplate." Wikler added that such thinking is indicative of a broader problem that makes Democrats less susceptible to pressure from their left than Republicans are to pressure from their right. "It reflects a structural imbalance in the way that media incentives play out across the two parties," Wikler said. "Reporters who seek to weigh both sides equally have influence only over Democrats. Republicans are playing to Republican partisan outlets, where any mainstream criticism is a badge of honor."[14] For this reason—and the others noted above—Democrats as a general rule are less inclined toward constitutional hardball than Republicans are.

But maybe Democrats *should* play more constitutional hardball. If Democrats perceive Trump and his policies as a serious threat to the country on multiple fronts—as they do—then don't the times call for much more hard-edged tactics? And once Democrats are back in control, shouldn't they take a lesson from the GOP approach and maximize their hardball playing in kind?

Toward a Realistic View of Democratic Norms

In their book, the aforementioned Harvard professors Steven Levitsky and Daniel Ziblatt argue that the norms of a functional democracy can be largely grouped into two categories. The first is mutual toleration, in which politicians accept the opposition as fundamentally legitimate. The second is forbearance, in which politicians exercise "self-restraint in the exercise of power." This involves refraining from "deploying one's institutional prerogatives to the hilt," even when so doing would be technically within legal and/or constitutional bounds—that is, it involves refraining from constitutional hardball. When these norms of mutual toleration and forbearance are eroded, it "alters the zone of acceptable political behavior." Both of these categories are intimately bound up with each other. To the degree that one side comes to view the other as illegitimate (eroding mutual toleration), the full exercise of power becomes more justifiable and tempting, and is demanded of that side's voters (eroding forbearance).[15]

The deterioration that we've seen on both these fronts has unquestionably produced undemocratic outcomes and outbreaks of serious instability. Ramped-up voter suppression tactics have disenfranchised untold numbers of people. Heightened gerrymandering (to be discussed in the next chapter) has produced unrepresentative electoral results. Debt-ceiling brinkmanship threatened the very real prospect of default and widespread financial destruction. The refusal to exercise congressional oversight—even as Trump has shredded norms of transparency and ethics in government—has facilitated his profiteering off the presidency to an untold degree, setting a terrible precedent for future abuses. The GOP enabling of—and active participation in—Trump's assaults on U.S. intelligence and law enforcement agencies to delegitimize the Russia investigation have harmed morale among the employees of those institutions and possibly weakened public confidence in the rule of law. And so on.

From this reading of what is happening, it would seem to follow that governing norms are inherently good things that should be maintained at all costs. If both sides simply refrain from pushing the envelope—if both sides refrain from constitutional hardball—the system would immediately function more smoothly and salutary democratic outcomes will follow.

But a number of progressive writers have mounted a powerful critique of this idea, arguing for a more nuanced view of governing norms, a more realistic understanding of their role in our history, and an unsentimental assessment of their utility going forward. At the core of this argument is the belief that it is a conceptual error to *automatically* identify the maintenance of norms with the preservation of a well-functioning democracy. Sometimes norm-*breaking*—or the full exercise of power—is essential for the sake of *improving and advancing* our democracy. Corey Robin, a leftist political theorist at Brooklyn College, illustrates the point by citing the Civil War, in which the total subjugation of the South through protracted and violent conflict was necessary to free the slaves and begin to right the greatest crime against democracy in our history. As Robin points out: "Sometimes democracy requires the shattering of norms and institutions," and indeed, "norm erosion" is sometimes "not antithetical to democracy but an ally of it."[16]

At the core of this claim is the idea that norms are not inherently good or bad. Instead, some norms enhance democracy, and others do not. Jedediah Purdy, a progressive

Duke University law professor, attracted some notice in the spring of 2018 when he argued, among other things, that the expansion of the franchise to vote over the centuries has itself required the bulldozing, usually through popular pressure, of once-existing democratic norms at various junctures throughout our history. As Purdy puts it, many of the movements knocking down barriers to voting have required the alteration, sometimes through violent struggle, of deep assumptions about who gets to be "active in the political community." Such successes, Purdy points out, all constituted "norm-breaking par excellence." For instance, for a good part of the twentieth century, our democracy's functioning rested on a consensus around exclusion of African American participation, which was in an important sense held in place by the observance of then-dominant norms.[17] Thus, if we accept that toleration of the legitimacy of the opposition and forbearance in the exercise of power are key norms that help democracy function, how do we reconcile the fact that the toleration of the steep barriers against African Americans voting put in place in southern states, and the forbearance from using federal power to overcome those barriers, constituted norms that ultimately had to be swept away to create a genuine democracy?[18]

In a similar vein, the law professors Josh Chafetz and David Pozen have argued that careful scrutiny will identify norms in the present that are destructive, such as the norm that politicians should refrain from labeling opponents' rhetoric or policies as explicitly racist, which could end up allowing subtly or structurally racist policies to escape serious criticism. Trump's explicit racism has had the effect of eroding that norm—it's now far more acceptable to call out that racism as such—which has to be seen as a positive exercise in norm-breaking.[19]

The bottom line of this critique is that a serious accounting of norms demands a careful effort to defend which are worth preserving and which are not—that is, which forms of constitutional hardball should be off-limits and which should not—and why. And predictably the questions of what forms of constitutional hardball are acceptable are themselves inevitably arenas for intense political contestation and will remain so. One might call this school of thought *norm realism*. Whatever position one takes in these debates, they will inevitably reflect deeper disagreements over what our democracy should aspire to be. And those disagreements are not going away. In fact, in coming years, they may become more pressing.

Is It Time for Democrats to Get Much Tougher?

It's a pretty safe bet that at some point in the future Democrats will be back in power, controlling one or both chambers of Congress, and by 2021, they may even control Congress and the White House. In anticipation of this, some progressive critics—let's call them *norm realists*—have argued that Democrats must be ready to massively escalate their constitutional hardball game. This means that Democrats must intensely study what the Republicans have done so well, with an eye toward closing the hardball gap. Closing that gap, these critics argue, will entail adopting a range of tactics. Once they have control of the Senate, they should get rid of the filibuster on legislation, making it easier for them to pass ambitious progressive legislation over Republican hardball efforts to block it. They must be ready to pass a new voting rights act, which would in effect negate state-level voter suppression laws by subjecting them to federal standards of some kind. Some have even suggested that the next Democratic president must consider trying to pack the Supreme Court, on the theory that if Democrats take the White House and Congress and begin to pass progressive laws, conservative justices will employ bad-faith legal theories in an ideological drive to thwart such democratic governance.[20]

Some or most of these things, of course, are unlikely to happen anytime soon. But in a sense, that's beside the point. The deeper argument progressives are making here is that Democrats need to shift their general attitude toward political combat in a very fundamental way. They have to accept that Republicans are going to continue to use maximal tactics for the foreseeable future, and if Democrats don't aggressively respond in kind, they will continue to put themselves at a disadvantage—for no good reason other than the maintenance of norms that only they are observing, which in effect renders them meaningless to begin with. Roosevelt University political scientist David Faris, the author of a book outlining this case that generated notice among progressives, puts it this way: "It's just not feasible for the Democrats to play by most of the rules—even the unwritten rules—when their counterparts across the aisle are not doing so." Faris adds that Democrats must match the GOP when it comes to "deliberate and pretty ruthless procedural warfare."[21]

For progressives making this argument, the push for Democrats to escalate their constitutional hardball is directly linked to their push for Democrats to adopt a much more ambitious progressive policy agenda. Their case is as follows: The problems gripping our democracy, exacerbated by Trump, cannot be analyzed in a vacuum. They are symptomatic of very far-reaching policy failings, particularly relating to the economy. Thus democracy is being undermined not simply by a deterioration of obeisance to rules and norms but by the policies that have produced excesses of unchecked capitalism. Soaring economic inequality and the unrestrained flood of big money in politics have enabled corporations and the wealthy to hijack the lawmaking process, paralyzing our political system's ability to respond to people's economic struggles. Flattening wages and the increasingly precarious plight of the middle class have hollowed out faith in government, opening the way for the rise of authoritarian populism on the right and a resurgent socialism on the left (captured here in the rise of Bernie Sanders).

And so serious, far-reaching democratic transformation, goes this argument, will require not just an improvement in the rules shaping the behavior of politicians, but also a policy agenda that breaks the hold of money on our democracy and inspires the mass voter mobilization necessary to push our political system to accomplish that goal. Precisely because such an agenda will encounter massive resistance from the Republican Party and its wealthy patrons, Democrats have huge incentives to dramatically ramp up their hardball tactics in order to genuinely reinvent and reinvigorate democracy. "If our republic's true sickness is its inegalitarian economic system," writes *New York* magazine's Eric Levitz, then "what's needed is a movement that mobilizes working people in numbers large enough" to effect "radical changes to the nation's political economy," which may require prioritizing the willingness to play constitutional hardball over any "nonideological commitment to procedural norms."[22]

A separate but related argument from these progressives is that an escalation of hardball is also directly linked to the urgency of the crises we face. For example, realistically responding to the threat of climate change would meet massive resistance from the GOP and its wealthy patrons. Therefore, only a combination of much more aggressive procedural tactics wedded to very ambitious policy solutions can stave off disaster before it's too late. Thus the willingness to employ hardball tactics in politics will—and should—be driven, at least to some degree, by your view of the moral urgency of realizing certain political outcomes or preventing other ones. Indeed, the political theorist William Galston has argued that under certain circumstances, a politician's values—and his understanding of his obligations to the country and to the people who have placed their trust in his or her representation—may *necessitate* pushing the procedural envelope and playing political hardball, even if it means resorting to "questionable, qualm-producing means." As Galston put it: "In most circumstances, a politician does not stand alone, but rather acts on behalf of others, or acts in ways that affect others, in pursuit of ends that others expect him to pursue." Becoming a politician says to your followers that "you take seriously the acquisition and maintenance of power and its employment to further the goals you share with them." This obligates the politician to assume the "responsibility to act effectively," which at times entails an "obligation to use the kinds of tactics a decent person will regard as intrinsically disagreeable."[23] (Interestingly, this is an argument that conservatives who want the GOP to play hardball to accomplish conservative goals might embrace.)

None of this is to claim that the political and policy ends should always justify the procedural means, but rather that any serious politics will inevitably run into the morally complex challenge of trying to determine when certain political and policy ends *actually do* justify particular procedural means. A recognition of these profound difficulties might be at the core of norm realism.

Is Fair Play Possible in Our Politics?

Or, to put the question differently, is there a way for Democrats to close the political hardball gap with Republicans in coming years, while also aspiring to an ideal of fair play in politics? Under my admittedly rudimentary theory of "norm realism" offered above, there is no simple way to resolve that question. Democrats will be pursuing two coexisting goals: winning policy and electoral battles in a time of escalating hardball and increasingly high political and policy stakes, while also ideally trying to move our politics toward greater procedural fairness. Is there any way to strike this balance? Is it worth bothering to asymmetrically strive for an ideal of fair play at all?

I believe they should strive for a complicated equilibrium, in which they do not unilaterally disarm in the face of Republican hardball, but also do all they can to make the system more rewarding for fair play. This entails three elements: First, be willing to escalate the constitutional hardball under certain circumstances, but only when it is seriously warranted, and only with care. Second, embark on a serious effort to determine which sort of norms are actually democracy-enhancing and thus are worth preserving, and which are not. And third, seek ways of bringing about a de-escalation of constitutional hardball on both sides that is genuinely mutual, by acting to take it off the table where possible. This means trying on multiple fronts to reduce the incentives and ability for Republicans to continue engaging in countermajoritarian tactics. What all of this would look like in practice is the subject of this book's final chapter. But first, we're going to take a brief excursion into one specific area in which these questions are going to be fought over in coming years with particular ferocity.

7

Total War: The Partisan Rigging of Elections

Imagine, if you would, the following scenario:

> It is election night. Democrats have won the national popular vote in the battle for the House of Representatives by six points, 53 percent to 47 percent. Yet Republicans still retain control of the House, because despite that deficit, the distribution of the national vote nonetheless allowed them to prevail in just enough individual House races to hold a slim two- or three-seat majority. President Trump's Twitter-thumbs spring into action, unleashing a volley of his trademark all-capital-letter tweets: "GREAT NIGHT FOR REPUBLICANS!!!" Never mind that Democrats actually won a fairly substantial voting majority in historical terms; right on cue, the TV blowhards fill the airwaves with insta-analysis, declaring the election a major repudiation of the Democratic critique of the Trump presi-

dency and a ringing public reaffirmation of the Trump agenda.

News flash, readers: This scenario is not far-fetched. It could very well play out in 2018. Or, if you are reading this after the 2018 election, one can envision a similar one in 2020, or even in 2022. It is a perfectly realistic possibility that in any one of these upcoming elections, Democrats could win the House popular vote by a sizable margin, but still end up in the minority, with Republicans in control of the lower chamber after the votes have been counted.

The reason for this is simple: Because of the way House districts have been drawn around the country, millions and millions of votes for Democratic candidates in House elections in effect are expendable. This is to no small extent by design—specifically, the design of Republicans who drew most of the lines shaping and defining those House districts in the last decennial redistricting back in 2010. This helped determine which voters are in each of those districts—that is, it helped determine the makeup of their electorates. In most states, the lines for House and state legislative districts are drawn by state legislators—the Constitution left it to states to determine how elections are held—and Republicans control far more state legislatures nationwide than Democrats do. This has allowed Republicans to rig great swaths of the electoral playing field in their favor, by drawing district lines with the explicit goal of degrading the value of Democratic votes and maximizing the value of Republican ones—and many of the voters who have essentially had their votes degraded do not even know it.

This is the state of affairs as we head into the 2018 and 2020 elections, but it could endure into the next decade if Democrats don't regain more influence over that redistricting process first. (District lines are redrawn every ten years, corresponding to the release of the census, and the next redistricting isn't until 2021.) Here's the reality: If Republicans retain a good deal of control over the process, they could redraw many district lines across the country to their own benefit once again, and the playing field could remain rigged in their favor deep into the next decade.

Democrats can take big steps toward reversing this conundrum. But first they have to reverse the massive catastrophic blunder that landed them in this fix in the first place.

Epic Fail

A lot is riding on the 2018 and 2020 elections—not just because control of the House and Senate is at stake, but also because they include state legislative and gubernatorial contests across the country. And those outcomes, by deciding who controls state governments, will decide who draws the electoral maps for the House and state legislatures in the next decade. One reason the stakes are so high in this regard is that the Supreme Court failed to step in and put a check on extreme gerrymanders when it issued two widely anticipated rulings in June 2018. The Court declined to embrace the argument of challengers who claimed that extreme gerrymanders—the most closely watched case was in Wisconsin,[1] and a related case was out of Maryland[2]—should be declared unconstitutional on the grounds that the gerrymanders had diluted the power of voters, by deliberately drawing lines to degrade their votes for the express purpose of entrenching their party in power. (It's worth noting that one of these gerrymandering challenges was from Democrats against Republican-drawn districts, while the other was made by Republicans challenging a Democratic-designed map—proof that both parties play this ugly game when given the opportunity. That said, Republicans are the ones who have pushed strategic cartography in recent years to far more indefensible extremes.)

Crucial to the dark art of gerrymandering—and to the argument against it mounted by the challengers—is the tactic of *wasting votes*. To do this, wily mapmakers carve up districts with a simple overriding goal: voters supporting the opposing party must be distributed to ensure that their party wins fewer seats, but wins them by much larger margins, even as the mapmakers' party wins more seats but by smaller (albeit still comfortable, "safe") margins. Thus, the opposing party's votes have been distributed in a manner that "wastes" them. If this is done successfully in an aggregate way, the overall percentage of *seats* the opposition candidates win will not keep pace with the overall percentage of *votes* they win.

How does this work? Picture a state of 1,000 people, made up of 500 Republicans and 500 Democrats, spread across four congressional districts, each composed of 250 people. Democrats are more concentrated in some areas than Republicans are, because Democrats tend to live in urban areas, but in theory, you could draw electoral borders with relative ease so that each district had an even number of 125 Democrats and 125 Republicans apiece. But what if you exploited the concentration of Democrats to draw a series of districts so that one district was packed with *substantially* more Democrats, leaving minorities of Democrats in each of the remaining three? District 1 would have, say, 200 Democrats and only 50 Republicans, so Democrats would be guaranteed to win that one district by a huge margin every time. But in Districts 2, 3, and 4, there would be 150 Republicans and 100 Democrats in each, enabling Republicans to win in all of those by comfortable margins—albeit not as big as the margin Democrats win by in District 1. The Republicans would have rigged the map to waste a whole lot of Democratic votes, enabling Republicans to win three out of four districts—comfortably, but not overwhelmingly—in an evenly divided state. This is a very extreme hypothetical, to be sure, but as we will see, the reality in some cases has also been shockingly outlandish.

As it happens, this cynical tactic is by and large perfectly legal, and in certain respects it represents a rational response to the system as it functions now. Partisan mapmakers on both sides are incentivized by the rules to try to maximize their own gains this way. Indeed, Democrats have their own long and sordid history of doing this, and in some states they have continued to do so. But in recent years, Republicans have pushed this tactic to new heights—or depths. Take the aforementioned case of Wisconsin. The GOP-drawn map allowed Republicans to win around half of the statewide vote for assembly candidates in 2012 and 2014 but at the same time win *nearly two thirds* of the assembly's 99 seats both times. Challengers to this cockeyed arrangement had hoped the Supreme Court would embrace a complex formula that would delineate when a gerrymander has deliberately wasted the opposition's votes to an unacceptable degree (as will be discussed in more detail below). But the court punted and put off any decision on the underlying dispute about whether such lines can ever be declared invalid. This preserved the status quo, leaving the parties largely free to keep on trying to rig House and state legislative elections to a maximal degree in their favor into the next decade. With Republicans in control of so many state legislatures and governorships—and over so much of the redistricting process—this means the pressure on Democrats to win back ground in the states is urgent and enormous.

The roots of this brutal political reality for Democrats can be traced back to a massive self-inflicted wound, as well as a spectacular confluence of factors that delivered a political bonanza for Republicans that they ruthlessly and nefariously exploited in a manner that continues to degrade our politics in all kinds of ways. That confluence is as follows. Republicans had the good fortune of entering into a midterm election in 2010, two years into the presidency of Barack Obama, when several crucial ingredients were in place. First, Obama faced the headwinds of the most horrific economic crisis in seventy years, meaning the backlash to his presidency was probably guaranteed to be a good deal fiercer than the backlash that historically pummels the party of the president in his first midterm. Second, that coincided with the decennial census, meaning that the state legislators propelled into power by that backlash would draw many of the House electoral maps in states across the country for the next decade. Those things dovetailed with developments in the technology of map drawing that made it ever easier to slice and dice constituencies for partisan advantage with mind-boggling precision.

The overconfidence of Democrats was another crucial factor, as party leaders appeared largely oblivious to that gathering storm. After Barack Obama's 2008 victory, Republicans seemed shattered, in total disarray, and severely on the defensive in the face of the inexorably changing demographics on display in Obama's victory at the hands of a popular majority of unprecedented racial diversity. The Democratic Party seemed solidly positioned to pass major progressive priorities into law and further entrench their majorities, and many prominent Democrats were preoccupied with the glamour of their takeover of Washington and with the task of setting about governing, as opposed to keeping their mind on the less romantic state-level contests to come. The failure to see the GOP's surprise strike coming was arguably one of the greatest strategic disasters presided over by the Democratic Party during the last decade. It helped pave the way for unbreakable GOP dominance of the House for most of Obama's two terms.

How Republicans Pulled Off the Rigging

You have almost certainly never heard of Chris Jankowski, a quiet, bespectacled, low-profile GOP operative who advises candidates in state-level races and consults for so-called dark money groups, which raise money from undisclosed donors, many very wealthy, for various causes that mostly help the Republican Party. Yet his hidden hand has left a mark on our politics that endures today. At a time when the GOP appeared plunged into darkness by Obama's stunning 2008 victory, Jankowski was one of the very first to recognize the potential for the GOP in developing a comprehensive national redistricting strategy. Pundits were declaring the GOP dead, but in July 2009, when the Tea Party opposition was just beginning to gain momentum, Jankowski helped launch an ambitious plan that would help engineer a much faster GOP comeback than most observers expected.

Jankowski's project was called REDMAP—an acronym

for Redistricting Majority Project—and it was run out of a GOP party committee devoted to winning state legislative races across the country. Jankowski helped raise $30 million from GOP donors by urging them to invest in a long-term strategy focused on under-the-radar battles for seemingly inconsequential state senate and state house seats, with the aim of winning GOP control of as many state legislatures as possible in the 2010 elections. Jankowski told donors that this would allow Republicans to redraw as many state congressional maps as possible after the 2010 census. If Republicans could win back the House of Representatives in 2010, while maximizing control of map drawing in as many states as they could, Republicans might be able to hold on to more House seats in subsequent elections, and hold their majority in the House for many years to come, creating an impregnable stronghold of opposition to the Obama presidency.

The plan was a spectacular success. As journalist David Daley recounts in *Ratf**ked*, his groundbreaking book about the redistricting wars, Jankowski and his fellow operatives targeted their spending with startling precision. They poured money into state legislative races in places where winning a handful of seats might swing control of the legislature, or into states that were set to gain or lose congressional seats due to reapportionment, which would mean the legislatures would have to redraw congressional maps from scratch, meaning the party that controlled the process could affect a total overhaul—one dramatically benefiting them, of course. It worked.[3] Not only did Capitol Hill Republicans win sixty-three seats and a large majority in the House; they won total control of twenty-five state legislatures across the country, to only sixteen for Democrats. Republicans controlled both the legislatures and the governorships in twenty states—including, crucially, in many of the largest swing states in the country.

And so, after the 2010 census, GOP-controlled legislatures redrew maps in Pennsylvania, North Carolina, Michigan, Wisconsin, Florida, and elsewhere—maps so brazenly rigged for Republicans that they helped shore up the GOP House majority through multiple subsequent elections. Because they redrew state legislative lines in their favor as well, Republicans further entrenched their control of state legislatures—and hence their control over district maps in many states. Making this even more of a disaster for progressives, this GOP takeover coincided with the radicalization of the party, leaving it determined to build a stronghold in Congress that would resist Obama at all costs. This successfully frustrated great swaths of the Democratic and progressive agenda.

How Rigged Is It?

The only way the Democrats can breach this GOP stronghold in the immediate term is in the event of a *huge* backlash to the Trump presidency in the 2018 and 2020 elections. There are two ways Democrats might do this. The first is simply by winning the House popular vote by a large enough margin to overcome the GOP's built-in advantage and win the majority (something that has become more urgent because of the Trump presidency). The second is by winning back enough state legislative seats to influence the next decade's redistricting.

To grasp the magnitude of the challenge to Democrats, consider that in part due to the success of GOP gerrymandering, in every election since 2010, the percentages of House seats won by Republicans nationally has been significantly larger than the percentages of the overall vote collected by Republican House candidates. In the 2012 election, 47 percent of voters nationally picked a Republican candidate for the House, and 48 percent picked a Democratic candidate. But Republicans won 54 percent of the seats to the Democrats' 46 percent. This was the first time since 1942 that a party lost the overall vote but still managed to win a majority of seats.[4] Two years later, in 2014, Republican candidates won the overall House vote by 51–46. But Republicans won 57 percent of the seats to the Democrats' 43 percent. In 2016, Republican candidates won the overall vote by 48–47. But Republicans won 55 percent of House seats to the Democrats' 45 percent.[5] (In fairness, it should be noted that the discrepancy between the popular vote and seat spread has long been a feature of our system, and Democrats have often benefited from it as well.)

Going into 2018, it is widely thought that in order to

net the 23 House seats necessary for Democrats to win the majority, their candidates overall have to win the national popular vote by at least six or seven points, meaning that they will probably need 54 percent. Hitting 52 percent or even 53 percent could still fall short of a House majority (hence the nightmare scenario sketched at the beginning of this chapter). Considering likely outcomes of the midterms, Nate Cohn, the elections numbers cruncher at *The New York Times*, noted that even if 2018 turned out to be a wave election in the Democrats' favor that rivaled previous waves, that would make them only "slight to modest favorites" for retaking the House, meaning they could benefit from a wave and "the Republican House majority could still survive."[6]

Here's another way to appreciate just how successful this Republican effort has been. Look at what happened in the states where the rigging was most brazen. Let's start with Pennsylvania. After winning the state's seats in the House of Representatives by 12–7 in the 2010 bloodbath, Republicans sought to lock in their majority in a way that would withstand future years in which the state's pro-Dem lean reasserted itself. The redrawn map worked brilliantly. In 2012, Obama carried the state against Republican Mitt Romney by 52–47 percent, and Democratic House candidates won slightly more overall votes. But Republicans nonetheless held thirteen House seats (one seat was lost to reapportionment), while Democrats were left with five. (A court has since ordered the creation of a much fairer map, and as a result, Democrats are expected to pick up several additional seats in the state in the 2018 elections.[7])

Or take good old North Carolina, another state aggressively gerrymandered by GOP mapmakers. In 2012, Democratic candidates for the House of Representatives won the overall popular vote by a couple percentage points, but Republicans won nine seats to four for Democrats. That edge held through the 2016 elections, in which GOP candidates pulled in a total of around six percentage points more in the overall popular vote than Democratic candidates did, yet Republicans won ten seats to three for Democrats, a much larger spread. In Michigan—yet another heavily gerrymandered state—Democratic House candidates overall in 2012 won a total of around five points more than GOP candidate did. Yet Republicans won nine seats to five for Democrats, an advantage that roughly held through the 2014 and 2016 elections. This pattern was also on display in Wisconsin, Ohio, and Florida.[8] In all these cases, wasting votes worked.

Yet for all this, determining just how rigged a gerrymandered set of districts is can be a complicated, thorny business. That's because the wizardry of mapmakers is not the only reason the playing field is tilted toward Republicans. For decades, a debate has raged among statisticians, political operatives, journalists, and political scientists over a very complex problem: What is the full range of factors that cause bias in district lines? The mapmakers themselves strive mightily to produce this bias in favor of their party, and often they succeed. But to what degree are their designs *alone* responsible for producing that bias? A whole school of thought has arisen around the idea that patterns of population distribution and the interaction of culture and geography are at least as responsible as conscious map manipulation is—perhaps more so—for this ingrained bias. In this telling, in recent decades, Democratic voters have inefficiently distributed *themselves*, by packing into dense urban cores and close surrounding suburbs, while Republicans are more efficiently distributed across larger expanses of exurban and rural territory. This, it is said, is a major cause of ingrained bias in favor of the GOP (which, again, turns on the idea that Democratic votes are wasted in overwhelming victories in fewer districts, while Republican votes are more widely distributed across more districts, which they win more narrowly, albeit still comfortably). These population distributions are ultimately an important cause of the problem, goes this argument, and GOP mapmakers are merely drawing lines that reflect already existing trends. Perhaps they are goosing the lines a bit in their party's favor where possible, but they are hardly responsible for those broader underlying realities.

That Democratic majorities are crowded into cities does, in fact, sometimes make it easier for Republicans to gerrymander. David Wasserman, the House editor for the nonpartisan *Cook Political Report* and one of the savviest data crunchers in Washington, illustrated the point for me by carving up Wisconsin into House districts on his computer screen as I looked on. First Wasserman created a map with a 4–4 split of Democratic-leaning and Republican leaning House districts. This mirrored the Wisconsin electorate, which is closely divided, so in this sense it was a fair map. Wasserman did this by splitting Wisconsin's two major urban centers, both of which are very heavy on Democrats—Milwaukee and Madison—in half, and putting each portion in a separate district, thereby creating four districts across the southern tier of Wisconsin, each with half of one of those cities and some outlying, more GOP-leaning areas in it. This spread the Democratic vote in such a way that it made it easy to divide the whole state into equal numbers of Democratic and Republican districts.

But then Wasserman played GOP mapmaker. With a few clicks of his mouse, he redrew the map so that all of Milwaukee and all of Madison were each in one district. This had the effect of packing all the Democratic voters in each of those cities into two districts, rather than spreading them across four. This is known as *packing*, and once those Democratic voters were inefficiently packed into two districts, it was easy to draw the whole map in such a way that the state's remaining six districts all tilted Republican, resulting in a 6–2 map in a closely divided state. The point, just as it was in our simple four-district example earlier, is that the inefficient sorting of Democratic voters actually does make it easier to gerrymander against Democrats, if Republicans want to exploit that sorting (which they very decidedly have). "In order to get Democrats to parity, you have to split cities," Wasserman told me.[9]

This inefficient sorting is a nationwide problem for Democrats. As Wasserman's calculations show, the median Democratic voter nationwide lives in a precinct where 65 percent of eligible voters are Democratic, while the median Republican voter lives in a precinct where 56 percent of eligible voters are Democratic. To be clear, this is at the precinct level—before any House or state legislative district lines are drawn—showing that across the country, Democrats are generally more concentrated, while Republicans are more spread out. This gives Republicans a natural geographic advantage, Wasserman says, which of course means a Democratic geographic disadvantage.[10]

Data nerds disagree vehemently about the degree to which that geographic disparity is responsible for the Democrats' structural disadvantages in the battle for the House. But here is one thing we can be sure of: Gerrymandering is certainly a partial cause of those disadvantages. Even Wasserman estimates that of the current GOP edge of twenty-three seats in the House of Representatives, probably around a dozen of those can be ascribed to Republican cartographical connivance.

Wasserman believes that if Democrats can regain enough ground on the state level to exert more control over the maps for the next decade in some of the big swing states, like Wisconsin, Ohio, and Michigan, and secure maps that are more in line with the popular vote spreads in those states, that could ultimately bring a dozen House seats back into the Democratic column.[11] That's a conservative estimate; other analysts think the number could conceivably be higher.[12] Needless to say, a dozen or more seats lost to gerrymandering is *a lot* of seats—and regaining them could make the difference in who controls the upper chamber.

An "Evil" as Old as the Republic

James Madison, as it happened, was among the first targets. Just after ratification of the Constitution, Madison ran for Congress, and his archfoe Patrick Henry, an opponent of the Constitution who badly wanted to scuttle Madison's career, sought to draw the lines of Madison's home district to exclude supporters of the Constitution—perhaps one of the earliest exercises of "cracking" in the republic's history. Madison prevailed anyway, thanks to his campaign vow to push for a Bill of Rights (which he subsequently authored) and extremely low voter turnout. It wasn't until 1812 that Elbridge Gerry, the governor of Massachusetts, gave *gerrymandering* its name by signing a law enshrining a district shaped like a salamander.

According to one early history of gerrymandering, by 1840 multiple states had grown familiar with the tactic. It attracted criticism early on, with multiple nineteenth-century figures and editorials lamenting it in terms that will sound very familiar to contemporary readers. James Garfield, speaking as a congressman from Ohio years before getting elected president, denounced the gerrymandering of his own state as an "evil." Garfield and many other critics pointed out the fundamental problem that remains with us today: Gerrymandering could be taken to indefensible extremes, but politicians could not wean themselves from the practice, since they benefited from it.

Federal courts had historically proven reluctant to police voting rules, including gerrymanders, but in the mid-twentieth century, the Supreme Court stepped in to revolutionize how district lines are drawn. Throughout the first half of the twentieth century, as cities swelled in population, the proportion of the numbers of voters in rural versus urban congressional districts grew more and more lopsided, diluting the power of urban votes and giving rural voters increased influence. In a series of rulings in the 1960s, the Supreme Court enshrined the principle of "one person, one vote," ruling that the Fourteenth Amendment's equal protection clause, among other constitutional provisions, requires electoral districts to be based on roughly equal population. The Court ruled that "each and every citizen has an unalienable right to full and effective participation" in the political process. This can be ensured only if each citizen has an "equally effective voice" in elections.

The now-mandated need for rough equivalence in the population of districts, of course, didn't stop state legislatures from continuing to draw lines to advantage their parties by wasting the opposition's votes. The question that the courts have faced since is whether district lines that dilute the power of voters by wasting their votes also constitute denying them an "equally effective voice." The Supreme Court has been willing to invalidate district lines that diluted the influence of voters along *racial* lines, as violations of the Voting Rights Act. But the Court has fractured over whether there is any "manageable standard" for determining when lines deliberately drawn to maximize the influence of one party's voters over those of the opposition has disenfranchised them in an unconstitutional manner. The Supreme Court has never invalidated a series of lines on the grounds that it excessively benefits one party over another, but Justice Anthony Kennedy had suggested in a previous opinion[13] that he might be open to doing this if a "workable standard" could be developed to determine when such an excess had been achieved.

In fact, the plaintiffs in the Wisconsin case had developed just such a measure. Nicholas Stephanopoulos, a law professor at the University of Chicago, and Eric McGhee, an electoral researcher at University of California, Berkeley, came up with what they called "the Efficiency Gap."[14] As we've discussed, maps that have deep partisan bias in them waste far more of one party's votes than the other's, allowing the advantaged party to win a percentage of seats that exceeds the percentage of votes it won. The Efficiency Gap measures this disparity. Through a complicated mathematical formula, it determines how many seats the advantaged party wins over and above the number of seats it *should* win, based on the number of votes, compared to a baseline that wastes both parties' votes in roughly equal numbers. For instance, if a map has an Efficiency Gap of +2 in favor of Republicans, that means Republicans won two seats more than they should have based just on the statewide percentages of votes. The higher that number, the more gerrymandered the map. In theory, the Court could rule, say, that a gerrymander deliberately drawn with no justification other than benefiting one party over time, with an Efficiency Gap of a certain threshold, is an extreme gerrymander and is thus unconstitutional. But it declined to do so, punting on the core decision and confirming that if there was ever a "workable standard" the Court could ever accept, it remains elusive.

Which brings us to where we are today. There is no telling whether the Court will ever police extreme gerrymanders (Kennedy's retirement may also make this even less likely, as will be discussed later) and that probably means we're headed for a major escalation in this tactic.

Total War Without End?

It might surprise you to learn that one person who is troubled by the prospect of such a massive escalation is none other than Chris Jankowski, the original mastermind of the post-2010 GOP gerrymandering offensive. When I met with him in the summer of 2017, at a pub near the White House, I was surprised to discover that he has grown somewhat chastened by some of the dark forces that have been unleashed by his strategy's success. In several conversations with me, Jankowski conceded that he has come to believe that in the wrong hands, redistricting can represent a genuine threat to fair political competition. He admitted that some of the maps of the previous decade have been absurdly unfair. Jankowski, of course, would know. He has spent years and years witnessing the process from the inside—meaning he has consulted with numerous mapmakers as they plied their sorcery, and he has dealt with the fallout when the process has gone awry, resulting in courts striking down maps or in public relations debacles that were successfully exploited by Democrats.

In our conversations, Jankowski declined to specify which state legislatures, in his view, had been self-destructively overzealous in rigging the maps in their favor, presumably because he didn't want to criticize his fellow Republicans. But it was easy to gather that he was talking about some of the extreme maps discussed above. He did not conceal his annoyance with some of the local mapmakers who, he said, had given the mapmaking trade a bad name, exposing his party to Democratic criticism that Republicans are trying to rig our democracy—which, he allowed, at times had some validity to it. As an example, Jankowski cited a TV segment on gerrymandering by John Oliver, in which the British-born late night political talk-show host cited some inadvertently revealing comments by a hapless state representative in North Carolina. District lines in the state had been struck down by a court as a racial gerrymander—meaning it had been drawn with the express purpose of diluting the influence of minority votes. In the course of drawing a replacement map required by the court, the lawmaker, Republican David Lewis, defended the new version by arguing, with startling candor, that it would be merely a *partisan* gerrymander, not a racial one. "We want to make clear that, to the extent that we're going to use political data in drawing this map, it is to gain *partisan* advantage," Lewis said. Oliver mercilessly lampooned these comments by scoffing: "The new map would not *illegally* fuck over *minorities*; it would *legally* fuck over *Democrats*."[15]

Jankowski told me that he now thought Oliver's comments perfectly captured a legitimate criticism of the manner in which practitioners of partisan gerrymandering defend it: "You're still admitting that you are doing everything in your power to use your office to benefit your party," he concluded.

Jankowski informed me that after seeing some of these abuses, he had come to believe that some kind of limits were necessary to prevent the process from getting flagrantly undemocratic. If he had his way, such limits might be put in place by state governments themselves—for instance, by passing laws that, say, used a standard such as the Efficiency Gap to create constraints on just how skewed maps could get. "We need guardrails," he insisted. (In a few states, courts have some oversight of maps, and around a dozen states have put in place commissions of varying kinds that help set them. Many voting rights activists are pushing for more commissions in the big swing states. We'll discuss this and other solutions in the final chapter.)

Certainly Jankowski was also speaking as a political operative—in warning for the need for restraint in the gerrymandering game, he was partly referring to the fact that maps overly gerrymandered by Republicans have backfired on them, meaning that if they're going to employ the tactic, they need to keep it subtle. But Jankowski's worries should be taken seriously. He noted that top Republicans are preparing for the likelihood that the Democratic Party's most experienced professionals will now be hyper-engaged in the next decade's gerrymandering wars. As such, he sees the potential for all of this to escalate without end. "There is an arms race quality to the whole thing," Jankowski told me. "It keeps escalating, and no one knows where it ends up."[16]

This escalation is now upon us.

We Won't Get Chumped Again

The Democratic Party has rushed to catch up with the GOP's redistricting successes by putting in place their own operation designed to take control of more maps in the next decade. The National Democratic Redistricting Committee is headed by Barack Obama's former attorney general, Eric

Holder, who has a long history of voting rights activism. Obama himself is quietly playing a behind-the-scenes role in raising money from the party's top donors. In a strategy similar to what Republicans did nearly a decade ago, as of this writing, the National Democratic Redistricting Committee and other related groups had budgeted up to $100 million to win back ground on the level of the states, with a focus on plowing money into places where victories might maximize Democratic influence over the redistricting process in the next decade.[17]

Yet here is the brute truth of the matter: The only way Democrats can reverse this tide in time for the next round of redistricting in the 2020s is by winning back an enormous amount of ground on the level of the states, very, very quickly. The party not in control of the White House has historically tended to win ground in the states, but during the Obama presidency, Republicans did so to an unprecedented degree. As of this writing, they fully control state legislatures in thirty-two states, while Democrats fully control them only in thirteen. There are thirty-three Republican governors to only sixteen Democratic ones.[18] Republicans have total control of the legislatures *and* the gubernatorial mansions in twenty-five states, to only seven for Democrats.

Among the states where Republicans either fully control the legislatures or control the legislatures *and* the gubernatorial mansions are North Carolina, Pennsylvania, Ohio, Michigan, and Wisconsin. As noted above, these are all states where Republicans *already* command extra House seats partly due to gerrymandered maps. Which means that, if Democrats can win back some control over the mapmaking process in those states, they can begin to unwind the GOP gerrymandering advantage in the next decade.

Because of their deep deficit, taking control of many of the legislatures is out of reach for Democrats in 2018,[19] but they have another play at their disposal. It is an often overlooked fact that in most states, governors can veto the maps drawn by state legislatures, which (if they belong to the other party) gives them leverage to block extreme gerrymanders and try to compel legislatures to draw maps that are fairer to both parties. (Another possibility is that in some states where Democrats install governors, they might gridlock with the legislature over the drawing of lines, throwing the process to the courts, which might also produce fairer maps.) There are three dozen gubernatorial contests in the 2018 elections, and around two dozen of them are unfolding in states that are currently held by Republicans, including the aforementioned Michigan, Wisconsin, and Ohio—states where governors have this power. If Democrats can win the gubernatorial mansions in places like that, it could make a real difference in what the congressional maps look like in the next decade.

And so, one legacy of the GOP's enormous success in gerrymandering this decade is that this set of rules defining our political competition—the lines that define the shape of congressional districts and determine how rigged our congressional elections are—is likely to be the subject of intense and brutal partisan conflict for the foreseeable future. Democrats, to be sure, have widely and repeatedly insisted that they only want to achieve fairer maps and don't want to engage in the type of election rigging employed by Republicans in the last decade. (Given that both parties have long histories of playing this game, Democrats as well as Republicans should be held to this.) Indeed, the National Democratic Redistricting Committee is also investing in ballot initiatives in multiple states that are aimed at installing nonpartisan redistricting commissions, which would theoretically produce maps that are fairer to both sides, as opposed to ones that are better for Democrats. We'll discuss this in the next chapter.

If we see nothing more than a major escalation on both sides, that is not likely to be a good thing for our democracy. As detailed in previous chapters, we're seeing intensifying white-hot polarization around other election rules, and this will only add to the fever pitch. Democrats cannot unilaterally disarm, and they absolutely should fight as hard as possible to unwind the Republicans' current rigging of the system. On that score, not gaining substantial electoral ground in the states between now and 2021 would be cataclysmic. But beyond battling their way back on that front, Democrats must also do all they can to prevent the redistricting wars from spiraling into a total war without end.

8

Conclusion: After the Trumpocalypse

First, the good news.

If you awoke on the morning after Donald Trump's election with a sense of foreboding about the future of American democracy, what we've seen since that dark day should in some ways be moderately encouraging. In important respects, our institutions have held up under the strain that the Trump era has inflicted on them. The free press has sustained its core independence and has produced a great deal of outstanding journalism exposing all sorts of Trumpian abuses of power. While there is still much work to be done in coping with the challenges posed by Trump's relentless lying amid a rapidly shifting information environment awash in gales of disinformation, key players appear to be thinking ambitiously about how journalism can retain a vital institutional role in our democracy as it transitions to a new and uncertain era. Trump's assaults on law enforcement and intelligence agencies and the courts, while very damaging, have not (as of this writing, anyway) decimated the rule of law or ongoing efforts to root out the truth about Trump campaign conduct during the 2016 election. Trump's nonstop attacks on our institutions and the legitimacy of our electoral system, rather than spreading civic apathy and demoralization, as intended, appear to have helped boost the political engagement of countless ordinary Americans. Important sociological fieldwork by Theda Skocpol and Lara Putnam,[1] and on-the-ground reporting by *The New York Times'* Michelle Goldberg, have demonstrated that all over the country, untold numbers of people who had been previously unengaged politically have poured "near supernatural energy" into many different forms of civic organizing designed to "rebuild democracy from the ground up," as Goldberg put it.[2] Trump has badly hobbled America's commitment to the ideals undergirding the postwar liberal democratic order, doing great harm to the international reputation of American democracy around the world, but that has been met with an outpouring of bipartisan calls for a renewed American commitment to its international leadership role as a (very flawed) exemplar of democratic values, suggesting the current damage can perhaps be mitigated in the post-Trump era.

True, the GOP Congress largely remains Trump's faithful enabler, effectively shielding his corruption from public scrutiny and accountability, and actively aiding and abetting his efforts to undermine the independence of law enforcement in the quest to avoid scrutiny and accountability.[3] But that abdication has left a breach that has been filled by an energetic response from civil society—that loose constellation of experts, nongovernmental institutions, and various other parties with a stake in making our political system work—who have risen up to combat Trump on many fronts. As E. J. Dionne Jr., Norman Ornstein, and Thomas Mann put it in their manifesto on the Trump era, the "renewed purpose and vitality" on display in civil society's response to the Trump menace has reminded us all of the "importance of organizations not directly linked to party politics" in "resisting government abuses and engaging more Americans in public work."[4] This has unquestionably been a hidden blessing of the Trump era. What's more, all this sustained pushback has constrained Trump in at least some key ways—it helped force him to back down (again, as of this writing, anyway) from removing the special counsel investigating Russian sabotage of the 2016 election on his behalf. The slide into autocracy has yet to materialize. There are reasons to believe our democracy will emerge in the post-Trump era somewhat less damaged than some observers feared. It is hard to look at the response to Trump without being somewhat heartened by the resilience of our political system and of the untold numbers of people who have been moved to action by the desire to do what little they can to protect and reinvigorate it.

Now for the bad news.

To return to the paradox outlined at the start of this book, it took a singularly menacing, authoritarian figure—

one who delights in flaunting his racism and profiteering off the presidency like a big middle finger unfurled in the faces of those who didn't vote for him, one who is openly contemptuous of liberal democratic institutions and all they have achieved—to rivet our attention on the state of our politics and democracy. But the problems eating away at our system predate Trump and, while they've been obviously exacerbated by him, will continue after he retreats to a private life of tweeting angrily at his television at five A.M. in his Trump Tower palace. Indeed, they may very well get worse. Yet when Trump is gone, too many of us will be tempted to take it on faith that everything is okay—that something resembling normality has been restored. This is especially true if Trump is somehow removed from office or if he is defeated for reelection in 2020. A great number of those infuriated by his rule will believe that a grand struggle over the future of our politics has finally been resolved in a dramatic and cleansing way, that a kind of rebirth has been achieved. However it happens, once Trump is gone, engagement may once again dwindle. But this must not happen. We have to figure out some way of bottling the energy and intensity of this moment—that renewed commitment to try to protect and revitalize democracy we're currently seeing everywhere—to channel it in democratically productive ways, and to sustain it after the Trumpocalypse has passed.

The Future of Polarization—from Terrible to Even Worse?

One of the bleakest depictions of our current plight—and of our political future—comes from University of Maryland professor of government Lilliana Mason. As noted in chapter 3, the extreme polarization of our two political parties is to no small degree a story about race: In recent decades, the Democratic Party coalition has grown far more racially diverse, while the Republican Party coalition has remained overwhelmingly white. And as noted in chapter 7, geographic sorting means that Democrats are overwhelmingly packed into urban centers, while Republicans are more spread out across exurbs and rural areas. Mason posits that in addition to this racial and geographic divergence, the two parties are increasingly sorting *along social lines* as well. Voters' partisan affiliations are increasingly bound up with overlapping social identities that include not just race and geography but also religion and culture.

The result is that the parties have become more and more socially homogeneous. Democrats, Mason writes, are now "firmly aligned with identities such as liberal, secular, urban, low income, Hispanic and black," while Republicans are now "solidly conservative, middle class or wealthy, rural, churchgoing and white." Mason marshals a good deal of social science to demonstrate that this sort of social sorting triggers group conflict instincts, in which these parallel identity-driven schisms are what shape each side's views of our political arguments, effectively blotting out any desire to resolve conflicts over issues in a manner that might better serve the common interest. This makes voters less inclined to revise false beliefs about the political opposition, and more inclined to see politics as a zero-sum struggle for "victory," which they increasingly crave at all costs.[5] If so, this would help explain some of the deterioration noted earlier in this book—that craving for victory fuels scorched-earth tactics and, with them, dramatically divergent realities when it comes to which side has demolished the possibility of fair play in politics. As Mason notes, these overlapping divisions of identity likely mean that the resulting deep and bitter polarization is not going away anytime soon.

Yet at the same time, the disturbing truth of the matter for Democrats is that the partisan *conduct* that results from that ongoing polarization will likely continue to be deeply unbalanced, with the two parties driven by a range of different incentives that lead Republicans to employ brutal and destructive tactics far more readily than Democrats do. In the previously mentioned[6] essay "Asymmetric Constitutional Hardball," law professors Joseph Fishkin and David Pozen also suggest that a combination of unbalanced factors—the insularity of the conservative media; the power of well-funded conservative groups; the threat of primaries from the right—will remain in place, resulting for the foreseeable future in a lot more destructive hardball from Republicans than from Democrats. That doesn't leave Democrats a lot of options. As Fishkin and Pozen conclude, they can "use temporary points of leverage to press for procedural changes that amount to *anti-hardball*," thus "taking certain types of constitutional hardball off the table."[7] To be clear, this does not mean Democrats should unilaterally disarm. Rather, it means Democrats will have to do whatever they can to, in effect, take the weaponry out of GOP hands (in effect, out of both parties' hands) wherever possible.

Democrats Can't Get Complacent

I mean this to refer to both capital-D Democrats (progressives and liberals who identify as Democrats, as well as party activists, strategists, officials, and lawmakers) and small-d democrats (people who want to contribute to the revitalization of our democracy going forward). We've discussed the stakes in 2018 and 2020, and the need for Democrats to remember the catastrophe that unfolded after their massive rout at the state level (as well as the loss of the House) imposed on them in 2010 only two years after their heady 2008 victory. As we've seen, that rout resulted in rigged electoral maps, an escalation of voter suppression efforts aimed at Democratic voters, and a fortress-like GOP House majority that employed norm-shredding procedural warfare that frustrated the Democratic agenda and repeatedly threatened serious harm to the country. So we've already seen how prone Democrats are to relax after triumph. But win or lose in the near term at the *federal* level, they must keep focused on winning ground back in the *states* for the foreseeable future, and this must remain a major party priority. As detailed in chapter 7, they have a great deal of ground to make up here, and it is going to be a long, hard slog.

This isn't just because controlling more governorships and state legislatures is inherently a good thing for the party. It's also because the states will be the arena in which near-term efforts to improve our democracy hold the most promise—and where the interests of capital-D and small-d democrats overlap. Those who want to see our democracy reformed—even if they are not necessarily Democratic partisans—have an interest in seeing Democrats regain more control in the states, because, simply put, Democrats are more likely to reform and improve our democracy than Republicans are.

Make Voting Easier

One reform that Democrats should pursue if they regain ground in the states is making it easier to vote. As detailed in chapter 4, automatic voter registration holds great promise. How this generally works is that states automatically add eligible people to the voter rolls when they interact with state government agencies (unless they opt out). This registration is ideally permanent and portable; when people move within states, they remain registered. Various versions of this have already been passed into law in a dozen states, but there is still plenty of fertile territory out there: None of the major swing states, save for Colorado, has done so. Voting rights activists believe that if Democrats can capture gubernatorial mansions in some of those swing states, such proposals might have a chance.

Yes, Republicans will likely continue to control legislative chambers in many of those states for the near term, making such reforms harder to achieve. But there are still reasons for some hope. If automatic voter registration is seen as a success once it gets going in the multiple states that have passed it, election officials elsewhere may see its virtues. This needn't be seen as a partisan reform: It has the capacity to improve the functioning of states' election systems, not only by making registration easier but actually helping combat the fraud that Republicans worry so much about (to the degree that it exists at all) by keeping voter rolls clean and up-to-date. It could also boost participation, and increased participation has the capacity to make people better democratic citizens and help them grow more informed.[8] Indeed, three red states (Georgia, West Virginia, and Alaska) are in the process of implementing this change—and a Republican governor signed a bill putting it in place in Illinois—which suggests at least the possibility that more Republicans could follow, especially if it works. As noted previously,[9] there are plenty of well-meaning Republican election officials who want to make voting more convenient for their constituents (even if some GOP lawmakers do want to make voting harder for those of them who vote Democratic). One could envision this reform bringing in more GOP-aligned voters, such as poor and working-class whites as well—something Republican officials should want. After all, isn't one of the lessons of Trump's 2016 victory—which may have relied on a larger-than-projected turnout among noncollege white voters[10]—that there is such a vast untapped pool out there?

Remove the Incentive to Rig Elections

Another thing that Democrats can continue to push for if they regain ground in the states is commissions that take the drawing of district lines out of the hands of politicians. In around three dozen states, the state legislatures draw the maps, and in most of those, governors have the power to veto them. But around a dozen states currently have congressional district lines drawn by various types of commissions. There are political-appointee commissions, which draw and approve maps, and advisory commissions, which draw maps in a purely advisory capacity; generally, in both these cases, state legislators pick at least some of the commission members and the legislature must approve their plans for them to become a reality. Independent commissions, by contrast, consist of citizens picked by an appellate court or state auditor panel, and legislators don't approve the lines, so these go furthest in removing the drawing of lines from politician control. Those exist in their purest form in California and Arizona.

There are many variations among these commissions,

and this remains an area ripe for much more reform, so those who want to engage in activism on this front have plenty of opportunities. There are various pushes under way for referenda or legislation that would create such commissions in multiple states around the country.[11] The merits and demerits of such commissions and initiatives to create them have been the subject of much intense debate, and these matters are bewilderingly complex. But Democrats (capital-D and small-d alike) need to continually search for ways not just to make the drawing of these maps independent, but also for ways to improve the resulting processes so they better conform to standards of fairness that can generate broad agreement.

The bottom line is that people will always differ over what constitutes a fair map. No map can satisfy everybody. Somebody will always feel screwed. Somebody will always suspect partisan manipulation has seeped into the result. Politics cannot be removed entirely. But if this type of independent mapmaking is constantly refined and improved upon, broader public confidence in it can be achieved. Academics[12] and voting rights advocates[13] have suggested various ways to accomplish this, such as creating a process by which leading representatives of both parties have some sort of input into the final product, or by which commissions generate numerous maps that compete to be fairest to all concerned. The key guiding ideal here is that institutional processes can be made better through experimentation and good-faith negotiating, and when they are, they can channel the self-interest of many stakeholders with conflicting views toward constructive bargaining and compromise.[14] Neither party's politicians should choose their voters with the explicit goal of entrenching their own power, insulating their policies and leadership performance from popular accountability, and rendering the opposition's votes as worthless as possible. We can do better.

The Future of Extreme Political Hardball

In chapter 6, I argued that Democrats—faced with Trump's serial degradations, which represent an escalation of the long-running willingness of Republicans to play far more destructive political hardball than Democrats do—will face a delicate balancing act in the future. They cannot unilaterally disarm and must be prepared to escalate the hardball in kind, but only when it is seriously warranted and only with care. They must take seriously the task of deciding which norms are worthwhile to preserve and seek ways of deescalating the hardball by reducing the incentives for Republicans to engage in countermajoritarian tactics.

The seemingly endless disputes over partisan map-rigging and the ballot access wars provide places to start. Ohio State University legal scholar Edward Foley has persuasively argued that those two particular areas are very ripe for reform with an eye toward incentivizing the ideal of fair play in politics that we've discussed throughout this book. As Foley points out, excessive gerrymandering and voter suppression for partisan purposes constitute an active effort by one party to "capture the operation of the electoral process itself" to award the party an "unfair advantage" in the "competition to win votes." Foley describes this as an abuse of basic norms of fair play, which he distinguishes from foul play via extreme gerrymanders and voter suppression tactics by noting that the first constitutes "legitimate" partisanship, while the second constitutes "excessive" partisanship. As Foley notes, legitimate partisanship is a good thing: "appropriate" partisan competition is a "desirable feature of electoral competition" and a "healthy sign of political freedom." But foul play in politics perverts that into an "unhealthy . . . subversion of democracy" that "interferes" with the "authentic electoral choice that the voters would otherwise make."[15] In many cases, we don't know exactly where to locate the line between fair and foul play. But we usually know the latter when we see it. And the north star should be to disincentivize it.

Thus, if Democrats do manage to regain ground on the state level, as tempting as it might be, they must not play the mapmaking game the way Republicans did in the last decade. Instead, they should stand for judicious efforts to defuse such tactics on both sides—to the greatest extent possible. Liberal journalist Brian Beutler has argued that Democrats can extend the prospect of "mutual, permanent disarmament," via the creation of the types of independent commissions discussed above or other neutral mediating devices, offering this as an alternative to an escalation without end that will sometimes inevitably victimize Republicans.[16] On the voting front, Rick Hasen, the election law scholar at the University of California, Irvine, has suggested that Democrats should be willing to compromise by embracing some forms of voter ID—provided (and this is absolutely crucial) the provisions are drawn to avoid deliberately making it meaningfully harder to vote, and to offer genuinely easily available alternatives to those who might have trouble procuring proper ID. Such a trade would be in exchange for Republican support for efforts to make access to the ballot easier. Americans would almost certainly support this kind of compromise.[17] This can stand as a kind of perpetual offer of mutual deescalation, in which efforts to restrict access to the franchise are, in effect, de-weaponized as a tool for partisan warfare.

But at the same time, Democrats should keep pushing automatic voter registration where possible. Some Republicans may see this as an escalation of hardball tactics against them—an effort to rig the game in Democrats' favor and a breakdown in the sort of forbearance we discussed earlier, in which the party in power refrains from aggressively imposing its will on the minority party, to avoid severe harm to democratic relations. But if anything, this would actually represent a *careful* intensification. Marquette University political scientist Julia Azari has offered a useful way of distinguishing legitimate procedural escalations from suspect ones, noting that they primarily become problematic if they seriously imperil the independence of our institutions, represent flagrant abuses of institutional processes, or treat the opposition as fundamentally illegitimate, not when they merely represent the prevailing of one side in a legitimate political dispute, which is the lifeblood of politics.[18] Trump, of course, has carried out the former relentlessly, with Republican acquiescence, and as detailed in chapter 6, the GOP has engaged in far more of this kind of overreach than Democrats have. But pressing forward with reforms such as automatic voter registration would unquestionably be defensible. Democrats can try to make voting easier out of a sincere conviction that it will improve our democracy for everybody—which it would—even if it might benefit the party politically as well.

However, on another critical front, Democrats should exercise caution. If Democrats take back the White House and Congress, they will come under intense pressure to end the filibuster on legislation, making it easier to pass their agenda by a simple majority. Some will argue that Republicans didn't hesitate to play full-blown hardball (exercising indefensible secrecy; assaulting the legitimacy of agencies that provide lawmakers with neutral analysis[19]) to move their agenda when in power, so Democrats should play just as rough, especially if Republicans are standing in the way of majority rule. But Democrats should tread carefully—and paradoxically, the recklessness of Trump and Republicans is the reason why. As the 2016 election showed, in our hyperpolarized age, a hair-thin marginal shift in the electorate put full control in the hands of a madman president *and* a radical right-wing Congress. Any future progressive advances secured through the abolition of the filibuster on legislation could be abruptly undone by a bare GOP Senate majority. And as this era has showed, Republicans will not hesitate to rapidly overturn major legislative advances (see the GOP's failed effort to repeal the Affordable Care Act), no matter how carefully secured and no matter how much damage would be done to the country in the process. Political scientist Jonathan Bernstein has argued that if Democrats want to reduce the ability of the filibuster to frustrate majority rule, they can do so very carefully, by reducing the number of Senate votes needed to overcome the filibuster from 60 to, say, 55, thus preserving some insulation against the policy impact of abrupt electoral shifts.[20] This is what cautious escalation might look like. (Preserving the filibuster in some form might also sometimes force majority parties to at least try to tailor legislation to win over some members of the opposing party.)

Ending the filibuster on legislation entirely poses risks: It could make deeply destructive Republican reversals of progressive social legislation more likely later (not to mention make it easier for Republicans to impose future reckless policy changes of their own if and when they regain power again). Put it this way: If you are a progressive who wants to end the filibuster, you need to engage with this possibility seriously. One can envision scenarios developing that *might* make ending the filibuster appear more justifiable and urgent, say, if Republicans were to relentlessly filibuster one reform after another, despite pressing need and widespread public support. (To return to the "norm realism" of chapter 6, the urgency of the ends simply will at times make hardball procedural escalations, particularly retaliatory ones like this sort of response to relentless filibustering, appear more justifiable. There's no easy way to resolve whether or when this is right, which must be undertaken on a case-by-case basis, and will always be the subject of intense contestation.) But the point is that any such move must be undertaken with care, and with serious consideration of the consequences that would result if Republicans were to retake power in a post-filibuster world. If Democrats see GOP governance as extreme and destructive, then by their own lights they should feel obligated to act more judiciously when it comes to changing rules in a way that might assist their agenda in the short term but would threaten more long-term damage later. That may seem absurd, but it's the right thing to do for the country.

What about the Supreme Court? As of this writing, it appeared likely that Trump would succeed in getting a nominee to replace the retiring Anthony Kennedy confirmed before the 2018 election. Unfortunately, some legal scholars believe that a more conservative replacement for Kennedy could create new hurdles to democratic reform later. Kennedy seemed more open than the Court's more conservative justices to the possibility of a standard for declaring extreme gerrymanders unconstitutional; unlike them, he has voted to uphold the constitutionality of an independent commission to draw electoral maps (the one in Arizona) against legal challenge; and he is somewhat less hostile to the Voting Rights Act than they are. His replacement by a more conservative justice probably makes it less likely that the court will ever put checks on extreme gerrymanders; more likely that the Court might side with a future legal challenge to redistricting commissions, frustrating this reform; and more likely that it would uphold state voter suppression laws down the road. The prospect of a Supreme Court that further entrenches Republican countermajoritarian tactics will make the option of serious hardball against future Court nominees by Republican presidents look more tempting to Democrats, if and when they gain control of the Senate. If Democrats capture the Senate during the Trump presidency, similar scorched-earth tactics against another Trump nominee appear likely.

But here, too, we should be looking for ways to deescalate the warfare. Given that Democrats (should they take the Senate) would be expected to duplicate similar GOP tactics against a future Trump nominee, the process is at risk of further deterioration. As *Vox*'s Ezra Klein has pointed out, it is plausible that in "times when the Senate and the White House are controlled by different parties—which happens fairly often—there's almost no chance that any seat on the court will be filled," which is "an insane way to manage one of the most powerful institutions in American life." Because Supreme Court seatings are lifetime appointments, the stakes in any given nomination battle are extraordinarily high, since each enhances the possibility of one ideology dominating the Court across generations. In a period of escalating hardball, the result may be that it becomes "common for seats on the Court, perhaps multiple at a time, to remain open for years." A better approach—one that has been circulating for a long time, and has been championed by 2016 GOP candidate Rick Perry, who proposed a constitutional amendment to make it happen—is to limit Supreme Court tenures (Perry has proposed eighteen-year terms), with each president getting to appoint two justices, replacing ones that cycle out as they reach the end of their tenures.[21] Unlike packing the courts (discussed in chapter 6), which would cause further escalation, the overriding goal of this idea would be to at least try to ratchet down the stakes, rather than incentivizing the slide into increasingly extreme tactics. Yes, this is very unlikely to happen. But we need to think big.

Why We Should Think Big

A lot of smart people are thinking about all of the problems this book has discussed, and some of them advocate for big ideas in response. The group FairVote has proposed something called the Fair Representation Act, an ambitious reform that would, among other things, go to great lengths toward taking partisan map rigging off the table as a weapon of political warfare. It would replace our current winner-take-all district-by-district congressional elections with a new system in which we instead elect members of the House of Representatives by proportional representation, an approach used in many other major democracies. Under this system, instead of carving a state up into many individual districts, the state would be broken into a few larger districts, and each would have multiple representatives. Voters would cast several votes (ranking the candidates by their preference), and all of the top finishers would be elected. The idea is that even those who are in the minority in states across the country would get adequate representation. As political scientist and New America Foundation senior fellow Lee Drutman has explained, this would render gerrymandering largely useless (since you can't slice and dice the influence of the minority's voters away entirely). It would also make it a lot harder to "waste" the votes of people living in concentrated areas, which would help solve the problem of geographic sorting diluting the influence of voters and penalizing them for living in cities.

Such a system might also reduce the impact of both polarization and negative partisanship (in which voter preferences are driven by dislike of the other side), because it would create electoral space for more unorthodox Democrats and Republicans to get elected by minorities in the new districts (these candidates could appeal to crossover voters to pick them as a second or third choice). It could mean fewer safe seats and fewer lawmakers worrying only about primaries, not general elections (both of which help cause rigid partisanship and polarization in Congress, since there is little incentive for such lawmakers to compromise with the other side) and more competitive general elections.

All that, Drutman notes, could lead to "governing coalitions" in Congress that are "flexible" and "fluid," shaking up a system in which party leaders shape governing choices and enforce party-line positions with the primary aim of galvanizing the party's partisans and casting the other side as extreme in the eyes of a dwindling slice of swing voters. The result, Drutman says, would be a "system in which the incentives did not push political parties into zero-sum trench warfare, but towards compromise and coordination that would solve pressing public problems."[22]

Such a system would require a national change in the law mandating single-member districts, and it would shrink and alter the role of parties, so it's obviously a major long shot. But thinking big helps illuminate the depth of our problems, and people should not give up on the idea that major reforms are possible. Fairer representation is something we should strive for. It might succeed in turning down the volume on the hyperpolarization and negative partisanship, helping disarm ugly and undemocratic countermajoritarian tactics, make it harder for extremists to thrive, and incentivize moderation and constructive good-faith bargaining.

Meanwhile, some continue to advocate for various different sweeping national responses to problems like lackluster turnout and the devious partisan manipulation of voting rules. Leading Democrats—including Barack Obama and Hillary Clinton—have called for a national version of automatic voter registration, in which people would be automatically registered to vote in federal elections when they come in contact with a state or federal agency. Such national registration schemes might make some Americans (particularly those who distrust the federal government) uneasy, but the opt-out option might provide some reassurance to the suspicious. A number of Democrats have pushed for a restoration and updating of the part of the Voting Rights Act gutted by the Supreme Court,[23] so localities with a more recent history of voting discrimination would again need federal preclearance for voting law changes, a measure also supported by some Republicans.[24]

And then there is the Senate. Each state is represented by two senators, resulting in deep inequality of representation, since some states are far more populous than other ones. Because Democratic senators tend to represent states with higher populations than Republicans; the GOP Senate caucus represents many millions fewer Americans than the Democratic caucus does. Because changing this would require a constitutional amendment and is a virtual impossibility, David Faris has argued that Democratic lawmakers in California should consider breaking up their (very populous) state into as many as seven new states, each of which would gain two senators, most of whom would likely be Democrats (this could theoretically be done by the state's legislature and then made official by a future Democratic Congress). Faris notes that this, plus granting statehood to the District of Columbia and Puerto Rico (which would also add more Democratic senators), would ultimately give Democratic voters "the representation they want and deserve."[25]

But even if you don't view the imbalance in Capitol Hill's upper chamber through a partisan lens, the current arrangement still creates unequal representation. And it's likely to get worse: Due to ongoing geographic shifts, by one estimate, by 2040, the fifteen most populated states will constitute two thirds of the U.S. population but be represented by less than one third of the Senate.[26] It is often pointed out that the Senate is not supposed to be uniformly representative by design, but there's no reason why reformers cannot view the arrangement as something about our political system that is threatening to grow more undemocratic, and is thus a legitimate topic for reform.

It will obviously be up to California voters to decide if they want to initiate such a breakup of their state and this is of course very unlikely. But for our purposes, the point is that we should be thinking ambitiously, even if the ideas it generates seem unlikely to prompt action anytime soon. Indeed, one of this country's wisest theorists of democracy, Yale University's Robert Dahl—who passed away in 2014 at the age of ninety-eight—meditated on precisely this point in his classic work, "How Democratic Is the American Constitution?" Dahl believed that the Senate's makeup caused "gross inequality of representation," but despaired of the possibility of achieving a constitutional amendment to change it—or other undemocratic features of our political system—anytime soon. Yet he argued that there was value in debating such matters, anyway, because so doing would "invigorate and greatly widen" the public discussion of our system's shortcomings, which in turn would heighten understanding of its deeper deficiencies, and thus enlarge the public's appreciation of the "possibilities of change."

In other words, we should think big. We should not shy away from big arguments over our democratic future. Yet there's also a case for placing some faith in the possibilities of incrementalism.

We Can Make It Better

Because the Trump era feels intuitively similar to previous eras that we look back upon as exceptionally fraught moments for our democracy—from the McCarthy era to the tumult of the 1960s to Watergate—we naturally (and urgently) yearn for grandiose resolutions of the current tensions and problems. As noted in chapter 1, all this passion and anxiety has generated an outpouring of interest in the fate of our democracy—among experts and ordinary citizens alike—that is nothing like anything we've seen in recent memory. But this belief that we are living through an extraordinary historical moment—how true this is remains to be seen—in a sense carries its own dangers. As Dylan Matthews, a liberal journalist at *Vox*, has pointed out, it creates a romantic expectation for some sort of grand, dramatic conclusion that ultimately may disappoint us. Whatever is to be once Trump himself is gone—even if he is somehow impeached or defeated for reelection in 2020—his departure won't solve the many problems that this book has discussed. Those problems predate Trump, currently exist in tandem with his presidency, and will outlast him. But as Matthews notes, the craving for a great denouement risks "setting the standard for success impossibly high" when it comes to improving our democracy, thus breeding "disdain for good incrementalist ideas."[27]

But that doesn't have to happen, and it shouldn't. We can improve our democracy in all kinds of small but significant ways that could add up over time. We can work to unrig extreme partisan maps in one state after another, and to install neutral processes that will prevent such rigging over the long haul—not necessarily because this will help Democrats, though it might, but because it might edge the House of Representatives in a more, well, *representative* direction. We can work to make voting easier in one state after another—again, not necessarily because that will help Democrats, though it might, but more crucially because boosting political participation might make the electorate more representative in terms of race and income, which is a worthy democratic end in itself.[28] We can continue organizing around some of the national solutions mentioned above. We can work to clean up our disinformation-saturated discourse in all kinds of small ways. We can work to make journalism better by rewarding good reporting and finding more constructive ways to engage with it when it falls short. Bruce Bartlett, a veteran of the Reagan White House who has emerged as a vociferous critic of the contemporary Republican Party, has suggested numerous salutary ways we can all become better news consumers as well—by refraining from the pitfall of spreading disinformation ourselves and by cultivating news-consuming skills, such as learning to distinguish flimsy from solid sourcing, in ourselves and in others.[29] News organizations can find new and innovative ways to clearly inform consumers that they are being deceived by politicians, and to ferret out truth and communicate it via social media. Journalists and consumers alike can redouble their commitment to the profession's core values. All this could help contribute to a kind of feedback loop, weakening the grip of disinformation and official lies and reinforcing public confidence in the press as an institution that, at its best, is devoted to objective truth-seeking and plays a critical role in liberal democracy.

The chapters you've been reading are by no means exhaustive. The undermining of American democracy involves not just nefarious voter suppression schemes, rigged representation, and rampant, unchecked disinformation, but the corruption of the process by big money, and even (as we saw in 2016) an active effort by a hostile foreign power to interfere in our election on behalf of its preferred presidential candidate—a display of electoral sabotage that is expected to continue. But it is a good thing that no book that considers solutions can be exhaustive. After all, each day Americans from every state are working to come up with new ideas about how to make our democracy better.

These pages were intended as an exhortation to embrace the notion that improving our institutions over time, slowly and fitfully, through experimentation and difficult experience, holds out at least the chance of further tempering the power struggle of politics by channeling it into processes shaped around genuine, if imperfect and perpetually contested, ideals of fairness. That, in turn, holds out at least the chance that more and more people on all sides might more readily accept political outcomes—even ones that deeply disappoint or enrage them—as in some sense the product of fair play.

It may be that our current Thunderdome politics are such that most Republicans simply will never find common ground with Democrats on what constitutes fair play in politics to begin with. This may remain a point of profound and bitter contestation for the foreseeable future. But at times throughout our history, the most pitched arguments over the rules of our political competition have slowly given way to fairer resolutions when broad coalitions have come together to make it so.

In June 2018, the political world awoke to a remarkable Twitter thread in which Steve Schmidt, a lifelong Republican who worked on the campaigns of George W. Bush and John McCain, renounced his membership in the Republican Party, flatly declaring that the GOP has become a danger to our democracy—in effect, that it is no longer functioning as an actor in our democracy at all—and that the Democratic Party is "the only party left in America" that is committed to democratic values. It is easy to get overly sentimental about this kind of display—breaking with Trump's GOP is hardly a brave or lonely move these days—but it raises an important question: whether, amid all the hideous degradations of the Trump era, there are more Republicans out there who are willing to join in the pursuit of long-term reforms that will end some of the practices that seem so blatantly inimical to those values. We have witnessed some of this already—as noted in previous chapters, some Republicans have been critical of voter suppression excesses and the partisan rigging of maps, and many Republicans have joined efforts to make voting easier. How much more of it might we see?

We will eventually find out the answer to that question. But here's what we know right now: The only option is for all inclined to keep slogging away at it wherever possible, at the level of the states as well as on the federal level, and none of it will be easy. Even if some of these efforts are modestly successful over time, big, deep, and intractable problems will remain. If the history of democratic reform in this country tells us anything, it's that there will be plenty of brutal setbacks and reversals and backslides ahead—and a great deal of disappointment and despair. But if anything, all of this is an argument *for*, not against, keeping at it. And keep at it we must.

Acknowledgments

Thank you! This book would not have been possible if not for so many of you.

An enormous thank-you to my editors at *The Washington Post*, Fred Hiatt, Ruth Marcus, and James Downie, for their unflagging patience and support. A huge thank-you to my co-blogger, Paul Waldman, for stepping up and filling in so brilliantly in my partial absence; to E. J. Dionne, Jr., who has graciously supported my work and who continues to inspire so many readers and writers with his own; and to *Washington Post* fact checker Glenn Kessler, the most indefatigable tracker of Donald Trump's lies in the media today.

A big shout-out to the whole *Washington Post* reporting and editorial staff, led by Martin Baron, who put out a great and indispensable newspaper every single day. It is hard to imagine a better place to work.

A huge thank-you to the editor of this book, Geoff

Shandler, an extraordinarily perceptive reader who consistently found deft and innovative ways to elevate the quality of the text, and at the same time was somehow unflappable enough to put up with my kicking and screaming throughout this whole process.

A big thank-you to Lynn Johnston, my agent, who has been amazingly shrewd about this project and its potential throughout, and who talked me through its various stages in all kinds of invaluable ways.

Thank you to all the people who made the publishing of this book possible, especially Liate Stehlik, Lynn Grady, Andrea Molitor, Nyamekye Waliyaya, Vedika Khanna, and the whole team at Custom House, William Morrow, and HarperCollins. Thank you to Maureen Cole for promoting it creatively and tirelessly.

Thank you to Danielle Reed, an old newspaper colleague of mine from way back when, who had the out-of-the-blue idea to suggest me for this project.

Thank you to the many people who agreed to be interviewed for this book, sometimes repeatedly. Thank you to Rick Hasen and Ari Berman, who allowed me to access their wisdom, knowledge, and judgment on the topic of voting rights. Thank you to the analysts at the Brennan Center for Justice, who spent hours walking me through their research, and at the National Conference of State Legislatures. Thank you to Nick Stephanopoulos, who has devoted many years to unlocking the secrets to making our political system fairer, and who shared his insights with me with great patience. Thank you to Alexander Keyssar and Jack Rakove for their historical advice.

And my deepest thanks to my wife, Rachel, who has sacrificed more than I ever deserved to create a wonderful, meaningful life for our family, which is everything.

Notes

Chapter 1: A Dangerous Paradox

1. Aaron Blake, "Donald Trump Jr.'s emails about meeting a 'Russian government attorney,' annotated," *Washington Post*, July 11, 2017. Trump Jr.'s emails showed that he eagerly accepted a meeting (attended by other top campaign officials) with Russians on the grounds that negative information on Hillary Clinton supplied by the Russian government was on offer.
2. Greg Miller and Adam Entous, "Declassified report says Putin 'ordered' effort to undermine faith in U.S. election and help Trump," *Washington Post*, January 6, 2017.
3. Ashley Parker and David E. Sanger, "Donald Trump Calls on Russia to Find Hillary Clinton's Missing Emails," *New York Times*, July 27, 2016.
4. Glenn Kessler, "President Trump says the tax bill 'will cost me a fortune.' That's false," *Washington Post*, November 30, 2017.
5. David A. Fahrenthold, Jonathan O'Connell, and Anu Narayanswamy, "These are the GOP officials who have spent the most at Trump properties," *Washington Post*, last updated February 27, 2018.
6. David Choi, "Mar-a-Lago, the Florida resort where Trump has spent 25 days since taking office, sees huge boost in revenue," *Business Insider*, June 16, 2017.
7. James Griffiths, "Trump says he considered 'this Russia thing' before firing FBI director Comey," CNN, May 12, 2017.

8. Michael S. Schmidt and Julie Hirschfeld Davis, "Trump Asked Sessions to Retain Control of Russia Inquiry After His Recusal," *New York Times*, May 29, 2018.
9. Michael S. Schmidt and Maggie Haberman, "Trump Ordered Mueller Fired, but Backed Off When White House Counsel Threatened to Quit," *New York Times*, Jan. 25, 2018.
10. Greg Miller, Greg Jaffe, and Philip Rucker, "Doubting the intelligence, Trump pursues Putin and leaves a Russian threat unchecked," *Washington Post*, Dec. 14, 2017.
11. Nancy Bermeo, "On Democratic Backsliding," *Journal of Democracy*, January 2016.
12. Michael Coppedge, John Gerring, Staffan I. Lindberg, Svend-Erik Skaaning, and Jan Teorell, *Varieties of Democracy: Comparisons and Contrasts*, University of Gothenburg, V-Dem Institute, University of Notre Dame, Kellogg Institute, Dec. 2015.
13. Bright Line Watch, *Report on American Democracy*, May 1, 2018.
14. Bright Line Watch, *The Health of American Democracy: Comparing Perceptions of Experts and the American Public*, Oct. 5, 2017.
15. Pew Research Center, "As election nears, voters divided over democracy and 'respect,' " Oct. 27, 2016.
16. Public Religion Research Institute, American Values Survey, Oct. 25, 2016.
17. Bright Line Watch, *The Health of American Democracy.*
18. Pew Research Center, "Public Trust in Government: 1958–2017," Dec. 14, 2017.
19. Pippa Norris, "Is western democracy backsliding? Diagnosing the risks," available online at "Online exchange on 'Democratic Deconsolidation," *Journal of Democracy*, April 28, 2017.
20. Steven Levitsky and Daniel Ziblatt, *How Democracies Die* (New York: Crown, 2018).
21. E. J. Dionne, Jr., Norman J. Ornstein, and Thomas E. Mann, *One Nation After Trump* (New York: St. Martin's Press, 2017).
22. Robert R. Kaufman and Stephan Haggard, "Democratic decline

in the United States: What can we learn from middle-income backsliding?" http://pelg.ucsd.edu/14.HaggardKaufman.pdf.

23. Ibid, p. 28.
24. Robert C. Lieberman, Suzanne Mettler, Thomas B. Pepinsky, Kenneth M. Roberts and Richard Valelly, "Trumpism and American Democracy: History, Comparison, and the Predicament of Liberal Democracy in the United States" (Aug. 29, 2017). Available at SSRN: https://papers.ssrn.com/sol3/papers.cfm?abstract_id=3028990.
25. Emily Guskin and Scott Clement, "Poll: Nearly half of Americans say voter fraud occurs often," *Washington Post*, Sept. 15, 2016.
26. Public Religion Research Institute, American Values Survey, Oct. 25, 2016.
27. Ariel Malka and Yphtach Lelkes, "In a new poll, half of Republicans say they would support postponing the 2020 election if Trump proposed it," *Washington Post*, Aug. 10, 2017.
28. Kathy Frankovic, "Belief in conspiracy theories depends largely on which side of the spectrum you fall on," YouGov, Dec. 27, 2016.
29. Will Wilkinson, "How Libertarian Democracy Skepticism Infected The American Right," Niskanen Center, Nov. 3, 2017.
30. Jonathan Chait, "The Republican Court and Era of Minority Rule," *New York*, June 27, 2018.

Chapter 2: Voter Suppression

1. Jack N. Rakove, Richard R. Beeman, Alexander Keyssar, Peter S. Onuf, and Rosemarie Zagarri, amicus brief, *Arizona State Legislature v. Arizona Independent Redistricting Commission.*
2. Alexander Keyssar, *The Right to Vote: The Contested History of Democracy in the United States*, rev. ed. (New York: Basic Books, 2009), 20.
3. Ibid. For much of this account, I'm indebted to Keyssar's wonderful and rich history of the battles over the right to vote in America.
4. Julian E. Zelizer, *The Fierce Urgency of Now: Lyndon John-*

son, Congress, and the Battle for the Great Society, reprint ed. (New York: Penguin Press, 2015), 214.

5. Robert A. Caro, "When LBJ Said, 'We Shall Overcome,'" *New York Times*, Aug. 28, 2008.
6. The Brennan Center for Justice and the National Conference of State Legislatures both maintain comprehensive, up-to-date databases of voting laws in the states.
7. Samuel Issacharoff, "Ballot Bedlam," *Duke Law Journal* 64, no. 7 (2015).
8. This history is drawn from the National Conference of State Legislatures, "History of Voter ID," last updated March 31, 2017.
9. National Conference of State Legislatures, "Voter Identification Requirements/Voter ID Laws," last updated May 15, 2018. The National Conference of State Legislatures designates a voter ID law as "strict" if a voter without proper ID "must vote on a provisional ballot and also take additional steps after Election Day for it to be counted."
10. Wendy Weiser and Max Feldman, Brennan Center for Justice, "The State of Voting 2018," June 5, 2018.
11. Dara Kam, "Former Florida GOP leaders say voter suppression was reason they pushed new election law," *Palm Beach Post*, Nov. 25, 2012.
12. Aaron Blake, "Republicans keep admitting that voter ID helps them win, for some reason," *Washington Post*, April 7, 2016.
13. Patrick Marley, "Ex-GOP staffer says senators were 'giddy' over voter ID law," *Milwaukee Journal Sentinel*, May 15, 2016.
14. Richard L. Hasen, "The 2016 Voting Wars: From Bad to Worse," *William & Mary Bill of Rights Journal* 26, no. 3 (2018): 630–31.
15. Ibid., 635.

Chapter 3: Demographic Destiny

1. Emily Shapiro, "Trump: 'I'll keep you in suspense' about accepting election outcome," ABC News, Oct. 19, 2016.
2. Jenna Johnson, "Donald Trump says he will accept results of election—'if I win,'" *Washington Post*, Oct. 20, 2016.

3. Jenna Johnson, "Trump urges supporters to monitor polling places in 'certain areas,'" *Washington Post*, Oct. 1, 2016.
4. Philip Bump, "Donald Trump warns that 'other communities' are poised to steal the election," *Washington Post*, Oct. 11, 2016.
5. Nolan D. McCaskill, "Trump says illegal immigrants pouring across the border to vote," *Politico*, Oct. 7, 2016.
6. On Nov. 27, 2016, Trump tweeted: "In addition to winning the Electoral College in a landslide, I won the popular vote if you deduct the millions of people who voted illegally."
7. Public Religion Research Institute, American Values Survey, Oct. 2016.
8. See chapter 2.
9. Eric Lipton and Ian Urbina, "In 5-Year Effort, Scant Evidence of Voter Fraud," *New York Times*, April 12, 2007.
10. Justin Rood, "McCain Acorn Fears Overblown," ABC News, Oct. 16, 2008.
11. Lorraine C. Minnite, *The Myth of Voter Fraud* (New York: Cornell University Press, 2010).
12. David Corn, "SECRET VIDEO: Romney Tells Millionaire Donors What He REALLY Thinks of Obama Voters," *Mother Jones*, Sept. 17, 2012.
13. Jon Cohen, "Most are negative about Mitt Romney's '47 percent' comments," *Washington Post*, Sept. 26, 2012. The *Post* poll showed that nearly two thirds of Republicans viewed the comments favorably.
14. Alan Abramowitz and Steven Webster, "'Negative Partisanship' Explains Everything," *Politico*, September/October 2017.
15. Alan I. Abramowitz, *The Great Alignment: Race, Party Transformation, and the Rise of Donald Trump* (New Haven, CT: Yale University Press, 2018), 127–28.
16. Lipton and Urbina, "Scant Evidence of Voter Fraud."
17. Justin Levitt, "The Truth About Voter Fraud," Brennan Center for Justice, 2007.
18. Justin Levitt, "A comprehensive investigation of voter impersonation finds 31 credible incidents out of one billion ballots cast," *Washington Post*, Aug. 6, 2014.

19. Philip Bump, "There have been just four documented cases of voter fraud in the 2016 election," *Washington Post*, Dec. 1, 2016.
20. David Cottrell, Michael C. Herron, and Sean Westwood, "We checked Trump's allegations of voter fraud. We found no evidence at all," *Washington Post*, Dec. 2, 2016.
21. Richard A. Posner, *Reflections on Judging* (Cambridge, MA: Harvard University Press, 2013).
22. Samuel Issacharoff, "Ballot Bedlam," *Duke Law Journal* 64, no. 7 (2015).
23. Ari Berman, "Rigged: How Voter Suppression Threw Wisconsin to Trump," *Mother Jones*, November/December 2017.

Chapter 4: "This Dystopia"

1. Nolan D. McCaskill, "The 7 most inflammatory things Roy Moore has said," *Politico*, Sept. 27, 2017.
2. Jessica Taylor, "Roy Moore, Culture Warrior, Will Be Favored to Be the Next U.S. Senator from Alabama," NPR, Sept. 27, 2017.
3. Stephanie McCrummen, Beth Reinhard, and Alice Crites, "Woman says Roy Moore initiated sexual encounter when she was 14, he was 32," *Washington Post*, Nov. 9, 2017.
4. Kym Klass and Brian Lyman, "Turnout low after lengthy Alabama Senate campaign," *Montgomery Advertiser*, Aug. 15, 2017.
5. Mike Cason, "Turnout exceeds expectations in Doug Jones win in Alabama Senate race," AL.com, Dec. 12, 2017.
6. Benjamin I. Page and Martin Gilens, *Democracy in America? What Has Gone Wrong and What We Can Do About It* (Chicago: University of Chicago Press, 2017), 57.
7. Jan E. Leighley and Jonathan Nagler, *Who Votes Now? Demographics, Issues, Inequality, and Turnout in the United States* (Princeton, NJ: Princeton University Press, 2014), 4.
8. Miranda Green, "Obama invokes Nazi Germany in warning about today's politics," CNN, Dec. 8, 2017.
9. Obama's comments at the private fundraiser were shared with the author by a person who was present. Here's a larger excerpt: "When we don't vote, we lose. And so, our entire focus

has to be on how do we make sure that we are activating people, not just in a few places, but across the country to change our politics. And the final point I'm going to make is that we have a midterm election coming up that will be a test case, an opportunity for us to stop the bleeding, to restore a sense of hope and promise, to, in very concrete terms, save people's lives and make sure that they have health care and make sure that families are able to support their kids, that young people are able to get student loans. There are all sorts of concrete things, but it also gives us an opportunity to change the mood and reverse the narrative that somehow, we are moving into this dystopia where nothing is true and we just rage at each other, and the government can't function and chaos reigns."

10. Christopher H. Achen and Larry M. Bartels, *Democracy for Realists: Why Elections Do Not Produce Responsive Government* (Princeton, NJ: Princeton University Press, 2016).
11. Page and Gilens, *Democracy in America?*
12. Victoria Anne Shineman, "If You Mobilize Them, They Will Become Informed: Experimental Evidence That Information Acquisition Is Endogenous to Costs and Incentives to Participate," *British Journal of Political Science* 48.1 (2016), 1–23.
13. National Conference of State Legislatures, "Absentee and Early Voting," last updated August 17, 2017, and "Same Day Voter Registration," last updated May 27, 2018.
14. Leighley and Nagler, *Who Votes Now?*
15. Brennan Center for Justice, "Automatic Voter Registration," last updated April 17, 2018. As of this writing, the states that have approved automatic voter registration are Alaska, California, Colorado, Georgia, Illinois, Maryland, New Jersey, Oregon, Rhode Island, Vermont, Washington, and West Virginia. The District of Columbia has as well.
16. Rob Griffin, Paul Gronke, Tova Wang, and Liz Kennedy, "Who Votes with Automatic Voter Registration? Impact Analysis of Oregon's First-in-the-Nation Program," Center for American Progress, June 7, 2017.
17. Comments by Sam Wang at a conference on automatic voter registration organized by the Brennan Center for Justice, May 19, 2016.

18. Sam Wang, interview with the author.
19. Jeremy Bird, interview with the author.
20. Celinda Lake, interview with the author.
21. Donald P. Green and Alan S. Gerber, *Get Out the Vote: How to Increase Voter Turnout*, 3rd ed. (Washington, DC: The Brookings Institution, 2015), 157.
22. Ibid., 157–58.
23. Jeremy Bird, interview with the author.
24. Brennan Center for Justice, "Automatic Voter Registration."
25. Ibid.

Chapter 5: Disinformation Nation

1. Hannah Arendt, "Truth and Politics," *New Yorker*, Feb. 25, 1967.
2. Michael Schudson, "Belgium Invades Germany: Reclaiming Non-Fake News: Imperfect, Professional, and Democratic." This essay will be published in Schudson, *Why Journalism Still Matters*, forthcoming in November 2018 (Cambridge, UK: Polity, 2018).
3. Glenn Kessler, *Washington Post* database of all the false and misleading claims made by Trump since taking office, last updated on May 31, 2018.
4. Adding to the anxiety is Trump's reluctance despite insistence from White House and national security staff to use a secure phone.
5. Eli Stokols and Ben Schreckinger, "How Trump Did It," *Politico*, Feb. 1, 2016.
6. Thomas E. Patterson, "Pre-Primary News Coverage of the 2016 Presidential Race: Trump's Rise, Sanders' Emergence, Clinton's Struggle," Shorenstein Center on Media, Politics and Public Policy, June 13, 2016.
7. Mary Ann Georgantopoulos, "CNN's President Says It Was a Mistake to Air So Many Trump Rallies and 'Let Them Run,'" *BuzzFeed*, Oct. 14, 2016.
8. Margaret Sullivan, "Live coverage of a Pennsylvania rally was another free ad for Trump's favorite candidate: himself," *Washington Post*, March 13, 2018.
9. Glenn Kessler, "Trump Versus Clinton: The Pinocchio count so far," *Washington Post*, July 15, 2016.

10. Damian Paletta and Josh Dawsey, "Trump personally pushed postmaster general to double rates on Amazon, other firms," *Washington Post*, May 18, 2018.
11. RonNell Andersen Jones and Lisa Grow Sun, "Enemy Construction and the Press," Brigham Young University J. Reuben Clark Law School Legal Studies Research Paper Series No. 17-23, March 10, 2017.
12. Tony Schwartz, "I wrote 'The Art of the Deal' with Trump. His self-sabotage is rooted in his past," *Washington Post*, May 16, 2017.
13. Kelly Field, "What Reality TV Taught Trump, According to Professors Who Study It," *Chronicle of Higher Education*, Feb. 15, 2017.
14. Jacob T. Levy, "Authoritarianism and Post-Truth Politics," Niskanen Center, Nov. 30, 2016.
15. Jacob T. Levy, "The Weight of the Words," Niskanen Center, Feb. 7, 2018.
16. Quoted in "Hannah Arendt: From an Interview," *New York Review of Books*, Oct. 26, 1978.
17. Derek Thompson, "Why Do Americans Distrust the Media?" *The Atlantic*, Sept. 16, 2016.
18. Quinnipiac Poll, taken from April 20–24, 2018, showing that 53 percent of American voters trust the media over Trump to tell them the truth about important issues, while 81 percent of Republicans trust Trump over the media.
19. Brian Beutler, "Mainstream Media, Embrace Your Liberalism," Crooked Media, Feb. 8, 2018.
20. Amy Mitchell, Jeffrey Gottfried, Jocelyn Kiley, and Katerina Eva Masta, "Political Polarization and Media Habits," Oct. 21, 2014.
21. Matt Apuzzo and Sharon LaFraniere, "13 Russians indicted as Mueller Reveals Effort to Aid Trump Campaign," *New York Times*, Feb. 16, 2018.
22. Craig Silverman, "This Analysis Shows How Viral Fake Election News Stories Outperformed Real News on Facebook," *BuzzFeed News*, Nov. 16, 2016.
23. Andrew Guess, Brendan Nyhan, and Jason Reifler, "Selective exposure to misinformation: Evidence from the consumption

of fake news during the 2016 U.S. presidential campaign," Jan. 9, 2018. Online at: https://www.dartmouth.edu/~nyhan/fake-news-2016.pdf.

24. Alessandro Bessi and Emilio Ferra, "Social bots distort the 2016 U.S. Presidential election online discussion," *First Monday* 21, no. 11 (Nov. 7, 2016).
25. Soroush Vosoughi, Deb Roy, and Sinan Aral, "The spread of true and false news online," *Science*, March 9, 2018.
26. Isaac Arnsdorf, "Pro-Russian Bots Take Up the Right-Wing Cause After Charlottesville," ProPublica, Aug. 23, 2017.
27. Michael Newberg, "As many as 48 million Twitter accounts aren't people, says study," CNBC, March 10, 2017.
28. Scott Shane and Mike Isaac, "Facebook Says It's Policing Fake Accounts. But They're Still Easy To Spot," *New York Times*, Nov. 3, 2017.
29. Bessi and Ferra, "Social bots distort the 2016 U.S. Presidential election online discussion."
30. David M. J. Lazer et al., "The science of fake news," *Science* 359, no. 6380 (March 9, 2018).
31. David Lazer, interview with the author.
32. https://www.nytimes.com/2018/06/18/us/politics/trump-immigration-germany-merkel.html.
33. Craig Silverman, interview with the author.
34. Former *Wall Street Journal* editor-in-chief Gerard Baker made this argument in "Trump, 'Lies' and Honest Journalism," *Wall Street Journal*, Jan. 4, 2017.
35. Graham Vyse, "Why (Almost) Everyone Likes Jake Tapper," *New Republic*, March 9, 2018.
36. David A. Fahrenthold, "David Fahrenthold tells the behind-the-scenes story of his year covering Trump," *Washington Post*, Dec. 29, 2016.
37. Jay Rosen, "Winter is coming: Prospects for the American press under Trump," Pressthink, Dec. 28, 2016.
38. Brian Stelter, *Reliable Sources* newsletter, June 15, 2018.
39. Margaret Talev, then the president of the White House Correspondents' Association, gave such a speech at the White House Correspondents' Dinner in the spring of 2018. Martin Baron, the executive editor of *The Washington Post*, has delivered nu-

merous speeches along these lines, including the Oweida Lecture in Journalism Ethics at Penn State University, also in the spring of 2018.

40. Michael Schudson, "Is Journalism a Profession? Objectivity 1.0, Objectivity 2.0, and Beyond." This essay will be published in Schudson, *Why Journalism Still Matters*, forthcoming in November 2018 (Cambridge, UK: Polity, 2018).

Chapter 6: Is Fair Play Possible in Our Politics?

1. For a good brief summary of how this impulse played out across Trump's business career, see Tim O'Brien, "Donald Trump Wants You to Hate Robert Mueller, Too," Bloomberg.com, May 22, 2018.
2. The view that GOP voters tend to see things this way is held even by some Republicans. See, for instance, the quotes from GOP pollster Whit Ayres in chapter 3.
3. Mark V. Tushnet, "Constitutional Hardball," Georgetown University Law Center, 2004, http://scholarship.law.georgetown.edu/facpub/555.
4. Thomas E. Mann and Norman J. Ornstein, *It's Even Worse Than It Looks* (New York: Basic Books, 2012).
5. Joshua Green, "Strict Obstructionist," *The Atlantic*, January/February 2011.
6. Thomas Kaplan and Robert Pear, "House Passes Measure to Repeal and Replace the Affordable Care Act," *New York Times*, May 4, 2017.
7. Cristina Marcos, "GOP blocks Dem effort to request Trump tax returns," *The Hill*, March 20, 2017.
8. Glenn Kessler, "President Trump says the tax bill will 'cost me a fortune.' That's false," *Washington Post*, Nov. 30, 2017.
9. Nicholas Bagley, "President Obama flouted legal norms to implement Obamacare. Now Trump may go further," *Vox*, Feb. 1, 2017.
10. This was blocked by the courts, though the Supreme Court, which had only eight justices at the time due to the GOP refusal to grant Obama's nominee a hearing, deadlocked over the policy, meaning it might have been upheld if Obama's nominee had been seated.

11. Joseph Fishkin and David Pozen, "Asymmetric Constitutional Hardball," *Columbia Law Review* 118 (2018).
12. Matt Grossman and David E. Hopkins, *Asymmetric Politics: Ideological Republicans and Group Interest Democrats* (New York: Oxford University Press, 2016).
13. Fishkin and Pozen, "Asymmetric Constitutional Hardball."
14. Ben Wikler, interview with the author.
15. Steven Levitsky and Daniel Ziblatt, *How Democracies Die* (New York: Crown, 2018).
16. Corey Robin, "Democracy Is Norm Erosion," *Jacobin*, Jan. 29, 2018.
17. It should be noted that in *How Democracies Die,* Steven Levitsky and Daniel Ziblatt also make this point. They do not argue that norms are inherently or automatically good, and they argue that in the past, our norms have rested on a foundation of racial exclusion.
18. Jedediah Purdy, "Normcore," *Dissent*, Summer 2018.
19. Josh Chafetz and David Pozen, "How Constitutional Norms Break Down," *UCLA Law Review* 65, no. 6 (2018).
20. Jeet Heer, "How Democrats Can Over-Promise Like Trump," *New Republic*, May 11, 2018; Scott Lemieux, "Democrats: Prepare to Pack the Supreme Court," *New Republic*, May 10, 2018; Ian Millhiser, "Republicans are using long-forbidden tactics to chip away at judicial independence," ThinkProgress, Feb. 9, 2018.
21. David Faris interview with Osita Nwanevu, "Is It Time for Democrats to Fight Dirty?" *Slate*, April 12, 2018.
22. Eric Levitz, "America's Brand of Capitalism Is Incompatible with Democracy," *New York*, May 23, 2018.
23. William Galston, "Toughness as a Political Virtue," *Social Theory and Practice* 17, no. 2 (1991).

Chapter 7: Total War Without End

1. *Gill v. Whitford*, 2018.
2. *Benisek v. Lamone*, 2018.
3. David Daley, *Ratf**ked: The True Story Behind the Secret Plan to Steal America's Democracy* (New York: Liveright, 2016).

4. Sean Trende, "Why Republicans Lost the Vote But Kept the House," Real Clear Politics, May 16, 2013.
5. "Vital Statistics on Congress," Brookings Institution, last updated May 2018.
6. Nate Cohn, "California's Clues for the Nation: How to Watch the Primary," *New York Times*, June 5, 2018, and "What to Keep In Mind for Thinking About the Midterms," *New York Times*, April 26, 2018.
7. Nate Cohn, Matthew Bloch, and Kevin Quealy, "The New Pennsylvania Map, District by District," *New York Times*, Feb. 19, 2018.
8. In Wisconsin, in 2012 Democratic candidates for the House of Representatives overall won slightly more votes than GOP candidates did, yet Republicans finished with five seats to three for Democrats, a pattern that duplicated itself in 2016. In Ohio, in 2012 Republicans won twelve seats to four for Democrats, even though they won the overall vote total by a much narrower four points. (They won by much bigger margins in the next two elections while keeping that same seat spread.) In Florida, the GOP margin of seats far outpaced their vote share in 2012 (by 2016 there was a new court-approved map).
9. David Wasserman, interview with the author.
10. Calculations by David Wasserman, shared in an interview with the author.
11. David Wasserman, interview with the author.
12. The varied estimates here are driven by differences over just how responsible geographic sorting is for the Democratic disadvantage. Those who lean toward blaming sorting think it will be harder to draw maps that result in a great number of additional Democratic seats, even in states where the popular vote spread would seem to suggest that it's possible. But some analysts, such as Stephen Wolf of Daily Kos Elections, have experimented with map drawing and believe that the impact of sorting isn't that great and that maps much more in line with the popular vote spread are possible. Wolf estimates that gerrymandering may have cost Democrats as many as two dozen additional seats.

13. *Vieth v. Jubelirer*, 2004.
14. Nicholas Stephanopoulos and Eric McGhee, "Partisan Gerrymandering and the Efficiency Gap," Public Law and Legal Theory Working Paper No. 493, 2014.
15. *Last Week Tonight with John Oliver*, video published online on April 9, 2017.
16. Chris Jankowski, interviews with the author. In a subsequent conversation in the spring of 2018, Jankowski confirmed to the author that he still holds these views after the Supreme Court ruling that punted on policing gerrymandering.
17. Kelly Ward, executive director of the National Democratic Redistricting Committee, interview with the author.
18. The fiftieth governor is an independent.
19. Letitia Stein and Grant Smith, "Democrats fight for their future in tough statehouse races," Reuters, June 13, 2018.

Chapter 8: Conclusion–After the Trumpocalypse

1. Theda Skocpol and Lara Putnam, "Middle America Reboots Democracy," *Democracy Journal*, Feb. 20, 2018.
2. Michelle Goldberg, "The Millennial Socialists Are Coming," *New York Times*, June 30, 2018.
3. See the discussion in chapter 6 of the GOP Congress's role in blocking efforts to force Trump transparency and in actively joining Trump's efforts to undermine the Department of Justice investigation into Russian corruption of the 2016 election.
4. E. J. Dionne Jr., Norman J. Ornstein, and Thomas E. Mann, *One Nation After Trump* (New York: St. Martin's Press, 2017).
5. Lilliana Mason, *Uncivil Agreement: How Politics Became Our Identity* (Chicago: University of Chicago Press, 2018).
6. See chapter 6 for an extended discussion of asymmetric constitutional hardball and the differing incentives driving the two parties.
7. Joseph Fishkin and David Pozen, "Asymmetric Constitutional Hardball," *Columbia Law Review* 118, 2018.
8. See the arguments along these lines in chapter 4.
9. Ibid.

10. Nate Cohn, "Why Trump Won: Working-Class Whites," *New York Times*, Nov. 9, 2016.
11. The Brennan Center for Justice's website remains an invaluable resource for anyone who wants to catch up on these various initiatives and the local groups that are pushing them.
12. One leading academic who has urged such an approach is Stanford University political scientist Bruce E. Cain. See, for instance, his essay, "Redistricting Commissions: A Better Political Buffer?" *Yale Law Journal* 121, no. 7 (2012).
13. "Redistricting Commissions: What Works," Brennan Center for Justice.
14. For a forceful statement of this view in the context of redistricting commissions, see Cain, "Redistricting Commissions: A Better Political Buffer?"
15. Edward Foley, "Due Process, Fair Play, and Excessive Partisanship: A New Principle for Judicial Review of Election Laws," *University of Chicago Law Review*, July 2016.
16. Brian Beutler, "Democrats Shouldn't Seek Revenge for Republican Redistricting. They Should Offer This Deal Instead," *New Republic*, Aug. 27, 2014.
17. Richard L. Hasen, *The Voting Wars: From Florida 2000 to the Next Election Meltdown* (New Haven, CT: Yale University Press, 2012).
18. Julia Azari, "Forget Norms. Our Democracy Depends On Values," FiveThirtyEight, May 24, 2018.
19. See the discussion of Republican efforts to repeal the Affordable Care Act, and Republican threats not to raise the debt ceiling to force spending cuts, in chapter 6.
20. Jonathan Bernstein, conversations with the author.
21. Ezra Klein, "How to fix the Supreme Court," *Vox*, June 27, 2018.
22. Lee Drutman, "This voting reform solves 2 of America's most pressing political problems," *Vox*, July 26, 2017.
23. See chapter 2.
24. Republican representative James Sensenbrenner of Wisconsin is a cosponsor of one such bill, known as the Bipartisan Voting Rights Act of 2017.

25. David Faris, interview with Sean Illing, "Why this political scientist thinks the Democrats have to fight dirty," *Vox*, June 11, 2018.
26. Philip Bump, "By 2040, two-thirds of Americans will be represented by 30 percent of the Senate," *Washington Post*, Nov. 28, 2017.
27. Dylan Matthews, "The myth of an ending: Why even removing Trump from office won't save American democracy," *Vox*, April 23, 2018.
28. See the discussion of the research on all of these points in chapter 4.
29. Bruce Bartlett, *The Truth Matters: A Citizen's Guide to Separating Facts from Lies and Stopping Fake News in Its Tracks* (New York: Ten Speed Press, 2017).